Bird Count

Humphrey M. Dobinson

Bird Count

A practical guide to
bird surveys

Illustrated by Roy Wiltshire
and Robert Micklewright

Kestrel Books

KESTREL BOOKS
Published by Penguin Books Ltd
Harmondsworth, Middlesex, England

Copyright © 1976 by Humphrey M. Dobinson
Illustrations copyright © 1976 by Roy Wiltshire
and Robert Micklewright

First published in 1976
Published simultaneously in paperback by Peacock Books

ISBN 0 7226 5153 8

Filmset in 'Monophoto' Times by
Richard Clay (The Chaucer Press), Ltd, Bungay, Suffolk
and printed in Great Britain by
Fletcher & Son Ltd, Norwich

Contents

Acknowledgements

The publishers would like to thank the Director of the British Trust for Ornithology for permission to quote a number of results obtained from B.T.O. inquiries; the Editor of *British Birds* for permission to quote the description of the Little Swift on pp. 54–5; and the Controller of Her Majesty's Stationery Office for permission to reproduce the map shown on page 122.

The illustrations of birds on pp. 18–48 and 134–45 are based in part on material in the following books: *Longmans' Birds* by Humphrey M. Dobinson; *Oxford Book of Birds* by Bruce Campbell; *Sea Birds of Britain and Ireland* by S. Cramp, W. R. P. Bourne and D. Saunders; *A Field Guide to the Birds of Britain and Europe* by R. T. Peterson, G. Mountfort and P. A. D. Hollom; *Thorburn's Birds* by James Fisher; and *Flying Birds* by D. and K. Urry.

The illustrations of birds on pp. 18–48 and 134–45 are by Roy Wiltshire.

The views on pp. 60–61, 100–101, 110–11, 126–7, 148–9 and 162–3 are by Robert Micklewright.

Introduction

This book is intended to help anyone who is interested in finding out more about our wild birds in a methodical and thorough way – anyone who fancies making a study of our birds that will add a little, even if only a very little, to the knowledge we have of them.

Ornithology is a very attractive science because it is truly possible for an amateur to make a significant contribution, and, what is more, to do so without spending much money or going far from his home. The scientific journals are full of papers reporting the results obtained by such amateurs. The fascinating work on the behaviour of Great Crested Grebes by K. E. L. Simmons; the study of the decline of the Wryneck by Dr J. F. Monk and R. E. L. Peal; the exciting series of reports from the Wash Wader Ringing Group concerning the migration of waders from Siberia to Africa past our east coast; these are only a few of a host of papers that derive from entirely amateur work.

Many people are keen to take up ornithology, but unless they strike up a friendship with someone doing survey work, they may well find that their hobby remains purely casual – enjoying the birds they see, becoming more and more adept at finding them and recognizing them, but not actually contributing anything. Much of the information they need for taking the subject more scientifically is to be found only by those who already know the intricate routes through the ornithological literature, of monthly, quarterly, and annual journals, club and society reports, and £200 worth of reference books.

There is nothing wrong with the casual approach to ornith-ology, but there are many who seem to feel, as I do, that some-thing more methodical, more like research, makes the subject even more interesting. The song of a Blackbird is no less beautiful for knowing that a Blackbird sang in that hedge each spring for the last three years; but it is more interesting when you know that there are fourteen more Blackbirds on this farm (or housing estate or park) than there were three years ago.

But there is more to it than just interest for justifying encour-agement of the scientific approach. Birds reveal more quickly than almost any other form of living thing, the effect of our rapidly changing way of life on the environment – the results of the destruction of the hedgerows, of increased traffic, of leisure activities, of pollution, of insecticides, fertilizers, and selective weedkillers, of modern sewage disposal, clean streets and refuse tips. It is not that birds are more sensitive to these changes than men or mice or microbes; but they are easy to see, easy to study, and have a fairly short life-span. We must of course expect to see changes in the bird life – clean streets are worth the loss of Kites – but unless we notice the changes we will not be prepared to prevent catastrophes such as the contamination of our environ-ment by chlorinated hydrocarbons and PCBs. No one knows how many Blackbirds there are in Britain; but we have a much better idea now than ever before because a few hundred amateur ornithologists make sample counts every year. Similarly we can now detect changes from year to year in the number of eggs laid, fertility, and the life expectancy of the chicks. All these results are based on amateur observation.

I hope this book will help anyone interested to be able to make observations of this type, and to find groups of fellow ornithologists he can join if he wishes to. It is not a comprehen-sive course in ornithology, but it is my personal selection of a variety of topics that seem to me important, fascinating, and in need of methodical work. It is based on many years of experi-ence helping newcomers to develop these interests, and the choice of chapters accords with the topics we have worked on together.

Since so much of the material in this book is based on work I have done with others, there are many references to particular places and people. Three areas in particular are mentioned frequently: Cape Clear Island, in County Cork; the Nottingham area; and the Swindon area.

Cape Clear Island is the most southerly point of Ireland (except for the Fastnet Rock), and is a superb place for sea-watching and for finding rare birds on migration. I was one of the team of five that established a bird observatory there in 1959, and worked for years building it up. Nottingham and Swindon feature in this book because I have taught at schools there, and in both of the schools I have run an ornithological club. The club at Fairham School, Nottingham, grew slowly at first, but then settled with about 120 members all actively engaged on the field-work that forms the basis of much of this book. The club at Dorcan School, Swindon, is still at an early stage of growth, but is working on similar lines.

Many pupils have undertaken a great deal of work and analysis that is quoted in this book, and in particular I would like to thank Nigel Balchin, Peter Barber, Nigel Bosworth, Terry Brown, Gary Goddard, Kevin Hemsley, Stephen Henson, Robert Malpas, Michael Peacock, David Southall, Terry Southall, Martin Sprosson, Michael Thompson, David Torr, David Walker and Paul Wilcox, along with any others accidentally not included, for all the hard work they have put into the surveys concerned. It has been a great pleasure to work with so many young enthusiasts. Special thanks are also due to my colleagues Stan Bullard, Brian Gadsby, Roy Nettleship and Richard Warren who, through many long hours of work with the Club, helped make all these results possible. Dr Tim Sharrock and several officers of the B.T.O. kindly read sections of the book in galley proof and corrected a number of points for me, for which I am most grateful.

1 Identification

Our great-grandfathers would have been astonished to see how good we are at identification now. Eighty years ago the only way to prove you had seen a rare bird was to shoot it. Even the Willow Tit, which was nesting over much of Britain, had never been identified. The ordinary field-worker had not heard of rare migrants like Icterine Warblers.

Our identification techniques have now improved immensely. This chapter suggests three stages to work through from being a novice to being really good at identification.

Half the fun of bird watching is being quite sure what sorts of birds you are looking at. Some birds look much like other species, and almost all birds are very good at teasing you by slipping away from view just before you have seen all the points you want to see. Some birds do not come out into full view, and you have to identify them from their calls only, or from what you can see of them as they fly fairly high over your head. Getting the identification right every time, and finding all the birds that are around, is a double challenge. Since the birds that are around are different every time, it is a challenge every time you go out.

There are so many species of birds to be found that when you are first taking up bird watching, it is difficult to know where to begin; some people are so disappointed when they cannot recognize everything straight away that they give up trying. It is important to accept that you must begin with recognizing the birds that are easy to see and easy to distinguish, and only come gradually to the stage where you try to put a name (and perhaps even more than a name) to every bird you see.

First stage: Recognizing sixty common birds

Many beginners are lucky enough to be able to go out bird watching with someone who can help them learn their first sixty species, after which it becomes much easier to sort out your observations for yourself. But if you have to go out on your own, go to places where it is easy to see birds close up. Although there may be a lot of birds in woods, they are very difficult to see there, or to watch for long. It is much easier to begin in gardens or in town parks, or else in farmyards and along country lanes, because in all these places you should be able to walk up slowly and quietly until you are quite close to the birds you are watching. It is not essential to have binoculars at this stage; in fact you might finish up as a better bird watcher if you begin without binoculars, but learn instead how to stalk birds without frightening them off, and how to spot quickly the points that help with identification.

While the bird is still in front of you, keep your eyes on it. Find out all you can about it. Look first of all for any really bright and clear patches of colour. Look to see if the bird has any patches of white, particularly on the sides of its tail, or on its wing, or over its eye, or on its rump. Try to see the bird's beak and legs: is the beak thick or thin? Are the legs long or short? Can you even see what colour the beak and legs are? What shape is the bird? Do you know any other bird that is about the same size?

You should look the bird up the moment it has gone. When you are past this stage it will be important to write notes first, and of course you might choose to do so even at this stage. But then try to match the bird with the illustration in one of the good pocket books. It is important to have a book with reliable illustrations and not too many species to look through. Probably the best three on the market are *A Field Guide to the Birds of Britain and Europe* by R. T. Peterson, G. Mountfort and P. A. D. Hollom, *The Oxford Book of Birds* by Bruce Campbell, and *The Observer's Book of British Birds* by S. Vere Benson.* The advantage of the first two of these is that the females and young are shown as well as the adult males; usually well over half the birds one sees are in these duller plumages.

In almost all modern bird books you will find the different species coming in the same order, called the Wetmore Order. It is thought that this is roughly the same order as the species evolved in. Quite apart from the advantage of always knowing where to look for a particular species, the Wetmore Order has the advantage of grouping birds in families. As soon as you can recognize a few species, you will begin to see the family likenesses which help so much in the later stages of more advanced identification.

Some notes are given on pp. 18–48 that might help you to spot quickly the most important points on sixty common species. For full descriptions of these birds you will of course need to look in the reference books.

*Full details of all books mentioned in the text are given in the List of Recommended Books on p. 187.

GREAT CRESTED GREBE

Where to look: Deep lakes, gravel pits.

What to look for: A silver-white bird with long neck and long beak, frequently diving. At close quarters ginger ear tufts and crest and darker back can be seen. Throat and under-parts gleaming white.

In flight: Rarely flies. Very narrow wings with white patches.

Call: Usually silent except a growl heard in spring.

CORMORANT

Where to look: Rocky shores, piers and harbour walls.

What to look for: A large oily-black bird with a long beak; white patches around the base of the beak, and usually on its side. It often stands with its wings out, drying them, keeping them still for a long time. Young birds can be foggy brown.

In flight: Large, dark, long neck, wedge-shaped tail.

Call: A low growl.

HERON

Where to look: Banks of slowly moving water, or wet fields.

What to look for: A large bird, dark grey above, pale grey underneath; long beak and long legs; neck may be stretched long and thin, or all hunched up so that you can hardly see it.

In flight: Very large, broad wings, slow wing-beat.

Call: Usually only calls if there is another Heron near by. An occasional deep-throated 'krarnk'.

Ducks

There are two main groups of ducks seen inland, the diving ducks and the dabbling ducks. Diving ducks have rounded backs with little tail showing, dabbling ducks have flat backs and some have distinct tails.

MALLARD (dabbling duck)

Where to look: Ponds and lakes.

What to look for: Male in spring has green head and reddish front, and it can always be distinguished by two curly feathers just in front of the tail. But in midsummer the male

goes into 'eclipse' plumage and this lasts until well into the autumn. At this time it is blotchy brown all over. Female is speckled brown all the year round. Beaks brownish or yellowish.

In flight: Both sexes show a blue flash with white borders.
Call: A short series of quacks.

TUFTED DUCK (diving duck)

Where to look: Deep water in lakes and gravel pits.
What to look for: The male is completely black except for white on the flanks and underneath; this shows up a long way off. In summer eclipse the male resembles the female, which is earth-brown all over except a small white belly patch.

In flight: Fast stiff wings, white patch near back of wings.
Call: A very quiet duck. You are unlikely to hear the occasional quiet growl.

Geese

Although geese can swim well, they usually stand about on grass. You can tell them from ducks by their upright stance and long straight necks.

CANADA GOOSE

Where to look: Town parks; often quite tame.
What to look for: Large, tall, brown, with black neck, white throat, black legs and beak.
In flight: Large, dark, slow wing-beat.
Call: A loud echoing honk.

Swans

The three species of swan found wild in Britain are all white; they are all very large with long slender necks. The young birds are brown.

MUTE SWAN

Where to look: Ponds and lakes, particularly in parks.
What to look for: A very large white bird with a reddish beak and a black knob above the beak. Black legs. Young birds are pale brown all over, and as they grow older more areas of white appear. It takes four years for them to become entirely white.
In flight: Listen for the air singing between the wing feathers.
Call: An angry hiss, or a quiet grunt. Young birds up to six months old have a babyish squeak that seems ridiculous in so large a bird.

BUZZARD

Where to look: In the sky above open country in the west and northern parts of Britain, and increasingly common elsewhere.

What to look for: A large bird with broad wings showing a pale patch underneath near the tips, circling and gliding with only occasional flaps.

Call: A mew somewhat like a cat's.

KESTREL

Where to look: Usually seen hovering above road verges or over open fields, especially near hillsides. Perches on telegraph wires.

What to look for: A fairly large bird (somewhat smaller than a crow), with long narrow wings and a long tail, often holding itself in one position in the air by flapping fast. Colours (brown and chestnut) difficult to see.

In flight: Shape of wings and tail is varied according to the wind. Kestrels can spread their wings and tails almost as broad as a Sparrow Hawk's in some weather conditions.

Call: Not often heard, a sharp 'kek kek kek'.

COMMON PARTRIDGE

Where to look: Open fields, usually fairly dry ones.

What to look for: A plump round bird, which may well look like a large lump of mud at a distance, and then may run like a clockwork toy. Red patches on the side of the tail, that show in flight, look like red legs but are in fact feathers.

In flight: Fast whirring wings, usually keeps low and flies fast and straight.

Call: Heard most often just before dark, a rasping 'crrick-ic-ic'.

PHEASANT

Where to look: Large parks, woods with thick undergrowth.

What to look for: A large heavy bird with a long tail. Males are reddish brown with a greenish head; females and young are speckled brown. Pheasants are often looked after by gamekeepers, and may interbreed with other types and so have unusual plumage patterns.

In flight: Takes off when you are very close to it, and rises suddenly with a great commotion. Flies low.

Call: A loud hoarse 'kark kark'.

MOORHEN

Where to look: Farm duck ponds, marshy streams, reed beds.

What to look for: A plump black bird with long greenish legs. Shows white patches under tail when it runs into cover. Often swims.

In flight: Moorhens rarely fly any distance. Very rounded wings, legs dangle.

Call: A loud 'kririck'.

COOT

Where to look: Deeper water in lakes and gravel pits, or grass banks.

What to look for: A bird that swims rather like a duck, but with an even more rounded body than a Tufted Duck, black all over except a white beak and white knob above the beak. Often dives.

In flight: Coots are hardly ever seen in flight except when scurrying across the water, splashing with wings and feet.

Call: A short sharp call in a rather high pitch.

Waders

Waders are birds that run in marshy places, often with their feet under water. When they fly most of them keep their wings very stiff, and flocks of waders often twist and swirl as they go along. Many waders are difficult to identify at the distance they are seen at, but their highly distinctive calls are a great help.

OYSTERCATCHER

Where to look: Coasts and tidal parts of rivers.
What to look for: A large black-and-white wader with red beak and legs.
In flight: Entirely black and white, stiff wings.
Call: A loud ringing 'kip kip kip'.

LAPWING

Where to look: Ploughed fields or rough grass.
What to look for: A fairly large bird with a shiny green back, a crest, and orange under the tail.
In flight: Squarish wings which are flapped in a jerky way, giving a flicker of black and white. Flight often wheeling.
Call: An enchanting 'pee-wit', loud and clear.

CURLEW

Where to look: Wet fields in the west and north, and muddy shores.

What to look for: A large brown bird standing high on long legs with a long curved beak, walking around and probing in the grass or mud. Usually in small flocks.

In flight: Fairly slow wing-beat somewhat like a gull's, but long beaks and white flash from rump up the back are distinctive.

Call: A beautiful 'cur-lee', and also a loud bubbling.

DUNLIN

Where to look: Muddy shores along tidal rivers.

What to look for: A small bird running along the mud. Fairly long black beak, grey-brown back, under-parts very pale, except male in summer which has black belly.

In flight: Thin white wing bar. Usually in flocks, which swerve and twist before settling again a little further along.

Call: A short rough 'chree'.

Gulls

Gulls are fairly large birds that swim often but can regularly be seen feeding on land. Adults of common British species are all white underneath, and the young are brown (for a few months in the case of Black-headed Gulls, and for four years in the case of Greater Black-backed Gulls).

LESSER BLACK-BACKED GULL

Where to look: Near the sea, tidal rivers, large gravel pits.
What to look for: A large gull, with a very dark grey back, almost black, yellow beak with red spot.
In flight: Slow wing-beat, curved wings.
Call: A deep 'ock ock ock'.

HERRING GULL

Where to look: Seaside, fishing ports, big rivers, town parks.
What to look for: Clear grey back, yellow beak with red spot.
In flight: Fairly broad wings: check the grey back.
Call: A ringing 'kow kow kow'.

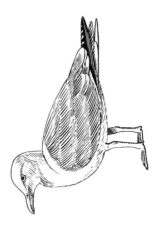

28

COMMON GULL

Where to look: Seaside, tidal rivers, fields.
What to look for: Pure pale grey back, greenish-yellow beak and legs.
In flight: Can only be distinguished from Herring Gull by smaller size and colour of beak and legs.
Call: Often makes a mewing note, a little like a cat.

BLACK-HEADED GULL

Where to look: Town parks, ploughed fields, refuse tips, seaside.
What to look for: Adults in summer have a chocolate-brown head. At other seasons look for a small black spot behind the eye on a white head. At all seasons look for red beak and legs.
In flight: Clear white band across leading edge of wings.
Call: A harsh 'kwair, kwair'.

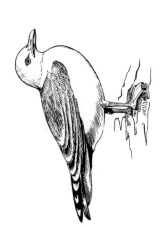

Doves and Pigeons

There are two groups of doves wild in Britain. Wood-pigeons, feral pigeons (racing pigeons that have gone wild), and Stock Doves are plump birds with short thick legs. Collared Doves and Turtle Doves are longer and slenderer but also have short thick legs.

WOODPIGEON

Where to look: Parks, cornfields, fields with clover or greens, woods.
What to look for: A large bird, mostly grey, with some pink on the breast.
In flight: Clear white wing patches near shoulders.
Call: Five coos in a row, the middle one being longest and loudest: coo-coo-*cooo*-coo-cu.

COLLARED DOVE

Where to look: Farmyards, hen runs, town parks.
What to look for: A long slender creamy-brown bird with a small black line on the collar.
In flight: Broad white band under tail, with black further up.
Call: Three coos in a row, the middle one loudest and longest: coo-*cooo*-cu. Also often makes a whirring noise in display flight.

CUCKOO

Where to look: Open country.

What to look for: A bird somewhat like a Kestrel in size and shape, but perches with wings and tail drooping a little. Bluish-grey, with clear bars across breast. White spots on tail.

In flight: Long wings and tail resemble Kestrel, but the wings never rise above the body line, and flight is usually fairly low and weak.

Call: A distinctive ringing 'cuckoo' in May and early June, less often heard later. Bubbling note of female heard more in midsummer. Do not confuse a Cuckoo with a distant Woodpigeon – the pigeon's note is softer and has more coos.

TAWNY OWL

Where to look: Around old trees with holes in.

What to look for: A large mottled brown bird with legs and neck hardly noticeable, perched in a very upright position. Main colour similar to tree bark or rather dark earth.

In flight: Silent flight, usually rather low, curved wings, mostly seen around dusk.

Call: A double hoot, the second part being longer, and a sharp 'ke-wick'.

SWIFT

Where to look: Always in the air except when coming to nest, which is built below roofs of Victorian buildings, in church towers and other old tall buildings. Seen in town and country.

What to look for: Almost entirely sooty black, with long incredibly narrow wings forming an almost perfect semicircle, and a long narrow body behind the wings, almost no head projecting forwards.

Call: A high-pitched scream.

KINGFISHER

Where to look: Running streams where minnows, small trout, or other small fish can be found.

What to look for: You are most likely to see the Kingfisher in flight. It goes fast, usually low, with fast wing-beats; it seems like a flash of blue going by. If you see it perched, you will see a salmon-pink breast and the shiny blue back.

Call: Rather quiet, not likely to be the first thing you notice; a high-pitched 'chik'.

GREAT SPOTTED WOODPECKER

Where to look: Woods with some dead branches. You may well be able to spot branches, or even fence posts, that have been pecked, before you see the Woodpecker.

What to look for: A bird nearly as big as a Jackdaw that climbs up trunks and along big branches of trees, often tapping lightly.

In flight: Bounding flight, big white patches flashing on wing. Short tail.

Call: Loud sharp 'kik' repeated several times. In spring you may hear the drumming (done with beak against branch) which lasts for several seconds and can be heard a kilometre away down wind.

SKYLARK

Where to look: Grass fields, or in the sky above them.

What to look for: A thick-set heavy brown-streaked bird. You may see the crest if you get a good view.

In flight: Song flight rises very high, and includes much hovering; usually comes down in steps, with a final dive. In long-distance flight closes wings every one or two seconds, and frequently calls 'chirrup'.

Song: May last for several minutes, usually made in flight.

SWALLOW

Where to look: Around farms, over ponds and slow streams.

What to look for: A blue-backed bird with long wings and long tail streamers, flying fast, with many twists and usually much chattering calling. Perches on wires.

Call: Twittering and chattering.

HOUSE MARTIN

Where to look: Often nests on houses that are fairly close to a pond or stream; feeds over ponds and streams, or in towns.

What to look for: Perches on wires as a Swallow will, but white under-parts and shorter tail distinguish it.

In flight: A House Martin can look rather like a fish in flight – silvery belly, dark back, but stiff wings beating fast.

Call: A rather buzzy 'chirrrup'.

CARRION CROW

Where to look: Big trees, grass fields, refuse tips.
What to look for: A large black bird.
In flight: Slower wing-beat than Rook. One of the slowest of inland birds.
Call: A fairly deep 'caw'.

ROOK

Where to look: Big trees, farms, ploughed fields, grass, often on motorway verges.
What to look for: A large bird, black at a distance, but inky blue if seen clearly. Adults have white skin around beak.
In flight: Slightly faster wing-beat than Crow, but nevertheless still quite leisurely.
Call: A pleasant somewhat ringing 'kah kah kah'.

JACKDAW

Where to look: Around old buildings, farms, old trees – anywhere with holes Jackdaws can go in.

What to look for: A fairly large black bird with a clear grey patch across the back of the neck, and a shorter tail than Rook or Crow.

In flight: Smaller than Rook or Crow, shorter tail, faster wing-beats.

Call: A loud quick 'Jack'.

MAGPIE

Where to look: Farms and lanes with thick bushes.

What to look for: A large bird, black and white at a distance, greenish-blue and white if seen well; long tail very striking, although for a brief period around August it may lose all its tail during moult.

In flight: Wing-beats seem weak, jerky.

Call: Loud harsh 'chack-a-ch-chack'.

GREAT TIT

Where to look: Gardens, parks, woods.

What to look for: A small bird, smart black-and-white head, yellow under-parts with black stripe, greenish back.

In flight: Rarely flies far; will usually perch and give good view after a short flight.

Call: Many different calls; a sharp 'chink chink' one of the commonest. Song a loud 'tea-t-cher tea-t-cher'.

BLUE TIT

Where to look: Gardens, parks, woods.

What to look for: A small bird, strikingly blue and yellow; blue around head and wings, with white cheeks; yellow under-parts, blue-green back.

In flight: As Great Tit, rarely flies far.

Call: 'Tsee-tsee-tsee-sit'. Song quieter than Great Tit, 'tea-cher, tea-cher'.

LONG-TAILED TIT

Where to look: Really thick hedges, patches of scrub land, or open areas in woods, where bushes grow.

What to look for: A very small bird with a long tail, moving along the bushes with short flights, settling on the ends of twigs, and often hanging below them. Usually in family parties of ten or twenty birds.

In flight: Weak fluttering flight, rarely going further than the next bush or tree along.

Call: A high-pitched whistle, a very short sharp 'pk pk', and a trilled 'tssrp'.

WREN

Where to look: Around old sheds, broken fences, or along streams.

What to look for: A very small bird, creeping like a mouse, flitting short distances, often cocking short tail right up; entirely brown, finely barred darker brown.

In flight: Only flies short distances, low down, with rapid wing-beats, diving into thick cover.

Call: A loud clear fast ticking. Song a loud high-pitched trill in three parts – a high trill, a slightly lower trill, and a high one again.

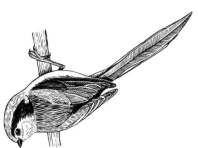

MISTLE THRUSH

Where to look: Playing fields, parks.
What to look for: A large faded brown thrush dragging its tail. Large spots on breast well spread out. White spots on end of tail get worn off sometimes.
In flight: White patches under wing. Quite a long tail.
Call: A loud rough churring.

FIELDFARE

Where to look: Playing fields, pasture land, big hedges with berries.
What to look for: A fairly large bird with a long tail, walking and probing in the grass, or balancing awkwardly on the top of the bush. Grey head and rump contrast with ginger back and black tips to tail and wings.
In flight: Long tail looks black and white, white under wing shows clearly.
Call: A harsh 'chack chack' and a musical note like a bugle.

SONG THRUSH

Where to look: Gardens, playing fields, parks.
What to look for: All upper-parts brown, under-parts paler with many spots on breast. Rather upright stance.
In flight: Orange under wing.
Call: A quiet 'sip'. Song often heard in gardens, can be very varied, but always repeats each bit two, or sometimes three, times, before beginning a new bit. A loud song usually given from a high perch.

REDWING

Where to look: Playing fields, pasture land, big hedges with berries.
What to look for: A bird about the size of a Song Thrush with a red patch on its side looking like smeared blood, and a white eye stripe.
In flight: Red patch under wing if seen closely. At a distance not easy to distinguish from Starling, but flaps more regularly, and tail very slightly longer and broader.
Call: A fairly thin 'seep'.

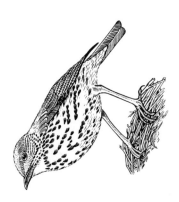

BLACKBIRD

Where to look: Gardens, parks, farms; probably Britain's commonest bird.

What to look for: Male is jet black, usually with a yellow beak. Female and young are dark black-brown with speckled breasts. All have moderately long tails.

In flight: Usually lands within view, often briefly cocking tail as a brake.

Call: Flies away with a loud 'chuck chuck chuck'. Warns others about cats with a metallic 'chink chink'. Sings a long varied song from high perches, television aerials, etc.

ROBIN

Where to look: Gardens, parks, farms, woods.

What to look for: Orange-red breast, clear brown back, long thin legs, rounded breast and upright stance.

In flight: Rarely flies far. Difficult to see red breast, so a Robin in flight looks like a small brown bird with rather broad wings and moderately long tail.

Call: A loud ticking, slower than a Wren's ticking. Song a series of short bursts of warbling.

BLACKCAP

Where to look: Rhododendron and other thick bushes in parks, woods.

What to look for: Male has black cap, female and young have chocolate brown cap; all are mouse-grey underneath, sleek, tidy and streamlined birds.

In flight: No distinctive features to be seen; a small rather uniform grey-brown bird.

Call: A very sharp 'tac, tac'. Song a long warbling, often including some very rich deeper notes.

WILLOW WARBLER

Where to look: Thick bushes, flowering shrubs, in autumn on the stalks of cow parsnip plants.

What to look for: A very small yellowish bird searching quickly over leaves and flitting from spot to spot almost like a butterfly. With a close view you can see thin beak, yellow eye stripe, sulphur-yellow breast.

In flight: Weak fluttering flight; wings more pointed than Chiffchaff.

Call: A sad 'poo-eet'. Song a gay trill down the scale, about eight notes long.

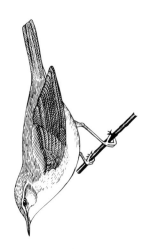

CHIFFCHAFF

Where to look: Tall trees, but, at migration times, much the same places as Willow Warblers.

What to look for: Cannot be safely told apart from Willow Warbler by sight alone except by very experienced observers. All Chiffchaffs have dark legs, some young Willow Warblers also have dark legs. Many books are misleading on this point.

In flight: Slightly more rounded wings than Willow Warbler.

Call: 'Poo-eet' note much as Willow Warbler. Song a monotonous 'chiff-chaff-chiff-chaff-chiff' repeated on and off for hours.

DUNNOCK

Where to look: Gardens with hedges, any areas with thick cover.

What to look for: An insignificant small brown bird, that creeps along the ground or sings from inside a low thick bush. While it used to be called a Hedge Sparrow, it is not a sparrow, having a longer thinner beak, a much more streamlined body, and thinner legs.

In flight: Rather rounded wings. Rarely flies far. Often flicks its wings excitedly on alighting.

Call: A quiet 'tseep'. Song a beautiful mixture of notes continuing for up to thirty seconds.

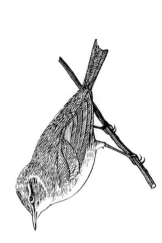

MEADOW PIPIT

Where to look: In summer, rough grass, moors. In winter, meadows, muck heaps, marshy areas.

What to look for: A busy small brown bird, heavily streaked, with white outer tail feathers.

In flight: Rises with 'zip zip zip' call. Level flight bounding, with a 'zip' call at each bound.

Song: Sings rising into the air like a Skylark, and then plunges down with wings and tail spread and a long-drawn-out note. Main song a twitter, less musical than Skylark.

PIED WAGTAIL

Where to look: Farmyards, mown grass, muck heaps, ponds.

What to look for: Male in spring almost entirely black and white. Female, male in autumn, and young, largely dark grey and white. Long tail often wagged, long wings, but the body quite small. Runs and feeds restlessly.

In flight: Can swerve suddenly to catch flies. Longer flights are bounding, with a 'chissick' call on each bound.

Call: 'Chissick', often repeated two or three times.

44

STARLING

Where to look: Towns, gardens, farms, muck heaps.

What to look for: A noisy bird, almost black with bold fawn spots, and a strikingly short tail; stiff wings and a powerful beak. Fairly long legs. Often feeds by probing into the ground.

In flight: Flies fast with stiff wing-beats followed by short glide. Short tail distinctive.

Call: Loud, almost human, whistles. Also a rude 'tcheer'.

GREENFINCH

Where to look: Waste ground with weed seeds; thick hedges; gardens with peanuts put out.

What to look for: A stocky bird with a heavy beak and yellow edges on the wing and tail. While the male in summer is yellowish-green over most of his body, females, young and many males are more streaked brown with only a trace of yellow or green except the wing and tail patches. Tail is notched.

In flight: Broad wings, short notched tail; yellow wing patches should be visible. Chattery call.

Call: A harsh chatter; a whistling 'tsoo-eet'; and a song often made in a zig-zag flight which is a mixture of a twitter and these call notes.

GOLDFINCH

Where to look: Apple trees; thistles gone to seed; waste ground with weed seed.

What to look for: A gaily coloured small bird with golden patches on the wing, and a crimson patch around the base of the beak. Back ginger brown.

In flight: Golden patches flash clearly; pale rump; notched tail.

Call: A musical twitter, given most of the time while feeding and in flight.

LINNET

Where to look: Rough bushes, anywhere with weed seeds.

What to look for: Most Linnets are small streaked brown birds with some (but not always much) white edging on the wings and tail. Some males in spring can develop crimson breasts and foreheads.

In flight: Dodging bounding flight, often in flocks.

Call: A rapid twitter.

BULLFINCH

Where to look: Bushes and young trees, thick hedges.
What to look for: Males have plum-red breast and inky-blue back, white rump, black crown. Females have black crown, mouse-grey under-parts, white rump, black tail.
In flight: Weak flight on rounded wings. Rump patch easy to see.
Call: A weak whistling 'pweee'.

CHAFFINCH

Where to look: Gardens, farmyards, parks, big woods.
What to look for: Male a very brightly coloured bird, with deep pink breast, blue crown, greenish rump. Females mouse-brown with greenish rump. All Chaffinches have large white patch on forewing, together with white wing bar and white sides of tail.
In flight: Bounding flight with 'tsip' call at every bound.
Call: A ringing 'pink pink'. Song a rough trill down the scale finishing with a flourish.

YELLOWHAMMER

Where to look: Country lanes, farmyards.
What to look for: All Yellowhammers have ginger rumps and white on outer tail feathers. A stocky bird with a longish tail, heavily streaked brown, with a varying amount of yellow showing on breast, crown and belly.
In flight: Rump and tail feathers show well.
Call: A rather metallic 'tsip'. Song a series of short notes usually finishing with a long-drawn-out one, and often described as sounding like 'A little bit of bread and no cheese'.

REED BUNTING

Where to look: Marshes, reeds along water, occasionally on bird tables if near a canal or still water.
What to look for: Male in spring has glossy black head and white collar. At all other seasons Reed Buntings are rather sparrow-like birds, but more ginger, with white outer tail feathers, and rather more firmly streaked.
In flight: Usually only makes short low flights.
Call: A fairly quiet 'deu deu'. Song a monotonous 'zee zee zip' repeated at regular intervals every few seconds.

HOUSE SPARROW

Where to look: Houses, gardens, parks, farms.

What to look for: Male has grey head and black bib; female and young mouse-grey below, streaked brown above, with buff eye stripe and buff rump. Sparrows have thick beaks, dark brown or black (young have clear yellow flanges at sides of beak).

In flight: Rapid wing-beats and glides. Rarely flies far.

Call: 'Cheep cheep chip'.

For help with identifying seabirds (including Gannets and gulls; Kittiwakes and terns; Fulmars, shearwaters and auks; sea ducks and skuas), see pp. 134–45.

Second stage: Sorting out all the common birds

While the rough rule-of-thumb method described above may well be the best way of learning to recognize the first sixty species of birds, it is not a good enough way of observing to allow you to make accurate identifications of all the birds that you will see.

Before you can go out and be reasonably confident of making a correct identification of all the common birds, you must be good at two things: (1) you must know in advance what points to look for; to do this, you will need to read the reference books mentioned below; (2) you must be able to write good brief notes as soon as the bird has flown away and before you open the book to check the identification. More explanation on how to write brief notes is given below.

Reference books

Besides the three excellent books mentioned on page 17, you might like to look at some others at this stage. Two other pocket field guides are excellent, but have the disadvantage for the beginner of including a very wide range of species, many of which have never yet been seen in Britain. These are *The Hamlyn Guide to the Birds of Britain and Europe* by B. Bruun and *The Birds of Britain and Europe* by H. Heinzel, R. S. R. Fitter and J. Parslow. The *Pocket Guide to British Birds* by R. S. R. Fitter and R. A. Richardson is a useful book, including many of the birds that have escaped from captivity and have established themselves in a half-wild state in London parks and similar places. W. Reade and E. Hosking's *Nesting Birds, Eggs and Fledglings* is well worth studying, while you would do well to borrow from the library P. A. D. Hollom's *Popular Handbook of British Birds*, and, if you can get it, a copy of the magnificent book *British Birds* by F. C. R. Jourdain and F. B. Kirkman, now, unfortunately, out of print. There are many other bird books on the market but you can easily be misled if you try to learn about birds from many of the identification books that are on sale but are not listed in this chapter or on page 187.

While studying books indoors, look carefully for the points the authors make about distinguishing difficult species; look carefully at details of legs and beaks; check if there are eye stripes, wing bars or rump patches. It is useful to have a general idea about which birds are summer migrants, winter visitors, or birds of the seashore or mountain top, while remembering always that any sort of bird can turn up at an unexpected time of year or in an unexpected place.

Writing brief notes

While out bird watching, a small stiff-backed notebook and a pencil sharpened at both ends will be useful for any notes you have a chance to make. If you see a bird that you can recognize, try to study it long enough and carefully enough for you to add some notes in your book when it has gone away; it is especially valuable to note distinctive points that are not frequently mentioned in the field guides. If you see a bird that you cannot recognize, watch it as long as possible, and only write down your notes when it has gone away, or when you have seen so much that you can write a lot anyway. Later in this chapter you will find more details of how full-length field notes should be written.

The birds' mannerisms

The experienced observer often does not identify a bird by the striking colour patches at all, but by some special mannerism that the bird has. A wagtail's call, a Starling's flap and glide, a Lapwing's wheeling flight, may be quite sufficient for a final identification. Your own brief notes on species you can recognize should help to build up a store of points of this sort. Perhaps this list of questions will help to clarify what can be done:

● If the bird is calling, how long is the gap between each call? Some birds sing or call at such regular intervals that you can say a sentence or two between each call and stop just in time for the bird's next turn.

● If the bird is brown, what sort of brown is it? There are so many different browns in the world that the word on its own is not very useful. Is it milk-chocolate brown, sandy-earth brown, wet-mud brown, oak-bark brown, or cardboard-box brown? Try to be quite specific with any colour that you mention.

● If it is a water bird diving, how long does it stay under water? Does it come up near where it went down, or far away? Does it jump out of the water before diving, or just dip its head under and roll down? Does it make a splash as it goes?

● If it is a bird singing in flight, how long does it sing for? How high does it fly? How far does it parachute down?

● If it is a bird soaring in flight, does it wheel round or does it beat its wings? Or some of each? If it is circling up in a thermal (where hot air rises), does it go clockwise or anti-clockwise? Or sometimes one and sometimes the other?

● If it is a bird taking off, from land or water, how steeply does it rise? At 10°, 25°, 30°?

Angles of take-off

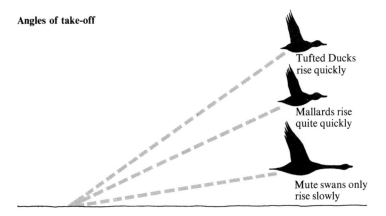

Tufted Ducks rise quickly

Mallards rise quite quickly

Mute swans only rise slowly

● If it is a water bird taking off, does it leap out of the water, or does it paddle along the top with its wings beating as it gains speed?

● If the bird is flapping and gliding, how many flaps does it make before a glide? If it calls, does it call at particular points in its flight, or all the time?

Here are some examples of the sort of notes that can be useful:

Kestrel: The wings came right down and to just above the horizontal. It had a chestnut back, longish tail and steel-grey wings. It flew straight and fast. 12.4.73.

Redshank: I saw a Redshank perching on a fence. I heard its call. It was a soft whistling 'teu'. When it flew I saw the wings were very stiff, the wing-beat was fairly fast and jerky. 1.5.73.

Goldfinch: I saw three feeding on ragwort. They clung to the weed, and then pulled each seed out, one by one. 10.4.73.

– NOTES BY DAVID WALKER

It is assumed that at this stage you are beginning to look for birds in places where it is much harder to see them well – along tracks in woods, around the edges of reed beds, on marshy shores and in big open places. With the help of book study and brief notes you should now be good at telling the difference between a Little Grebe and a Great Crested Grebe, a Stonechat and a Whinchat, a Marsh Tit and a Willow Tit, a Corn Bunting and a Reed Bunting, a Meadow Pipit and a Tree Pipit, a Turtle Dove and a Collared Dove. There is a lot of work at this stage; there are over 100 species of birds to be found fairly commonly in Britain, and your work ought to cover at least something about all of these. But as you get better at this, the chance of your seeing something really unusual increases. You will now be becoming a good enough observer to be able to note the points for identifying a rare bird reliably, and therefore you need to know how to record one if you have the luck to see it.

Third stage: Field notes on rare birds

If you are lucky enough to see a rare bird, you may want to report it, and to have the satisfaction of knowing that your record is accepted. There are a lot of people who think they see a rare bird, but they never record it properly, and no one else can ever be sure if they really did see it, or if it was in fact quite an ordinary bird and the observers had imagined various points about it – or even simply made a mistake. There is a standard procedure for dealing with all reports of birds seen in Britain, and if you follow this your record will be accepted if you have seen the bird well and made a correct identification.

Firstly, all records of birds that you see in your area, whether the bird is rare or not, will be of interest to your local bird Recorder. He or she will have been appointed Recorder by the local society (see details given in chapter 13). Since you would do well to submit all your records to the Recorder at intervals, you will probably have been in touch with him several times before you have the luck to see anything rare. This will certainly help in any correspondence that follows your sending in the record.

Whenever you see a bird that is rare in that place or at that time of year, you will need to write full-length field notes on it for the Recorder. If he is satisfied that you have seen the bird well and probably made the correct identification, and if it is a very rare bird, he will send the record to the Secretary of the Rarities Committee. They will then consider the record and will decide if it is acceptable or not. The 'ten rare men', as they are known, are particularly well qualified for making this decision: they have all travelled widely in the world and are outstanding for their knowledge of identification and for the number of species that they have seen in other countries. If you prefer not to

A particularly good example of a full-length field note was published by J. T. R. Sharrock in British Birds *in April 1968:*

Little Swift in Co. Cork: a species new to Ireland and Britain

On the evening of 12 June 1967, on Cape Clear Island, Co. Cork, I was sitting on top of a steep ridge overlooking Cummer, a narrow col situated between the north and south harbours. The soft evening light was directly behind me and it was perfectly calm. I was casually watching five or six Swallows *Hirundo rustica*, a House Martin *Delichon urbica* and five Swifts *Apus apus* which were hawking for insects through the col, when I spotted a swift with a gleaming white throat, contrasting with black under-parts. This bird passed several times about 10 feet [3 metres] above and 30 yards [27 metres] away from me. Other features distinguishing it from the Swifts were its shorter wings and less deliberate, more 'fluttery' wing-beats. The bird then flew lower, passing 30 feet [9 metres] below me and 60 yards [55 metres] away, and I saw that it had a very marked, square, white rump and that its upper-parts were a glossier black than those of the Swifts. I watched it for about five minutes as it hawked back-and-forth, sometimes below me and sometimes above me, but it apparently departed (along with the Swifts) while I was busy writing field notes, for only the hirundines were present when I tried to relocate it.

DESCRIPTION

The following details are derived from my field notes and sketches. *Upper-parts:* forehead appearing paler than rest of head, probably greyish-white; rump white, a large, square, gleaming patch like that of House Martin; rest of upper-parts less sooty, glossier and blacker than those of Swift. *Under-parts:* chin and throat white, a clear-cut gleaming patch larger than in Swift (the pale chins of the Swifts were not showing up in the same light conditions); rest of under-parts blackish, except for paler underwing. *Shape:* wings less pointed and shorter than those of Swift; tail square-ended and held more splayed. *Size:* smaller than Swift (difficult to determine with the birds flying at different heights and ranges, but particular attention was paid to this point).

Behaviour: did not associate particularly with the Swifts and came lower, sweeping over the ground at about 20 feet [6 metres]; wing-beats less deliberate than those of Swift and more fluttery.

IDENTIFICATION

The bird was clearly no swift on the British and Irish list and I suspected that it was *Apus affinis*. But the only reference to that species (under the now obsolete name of 'White-rumped Swift'), which was available at the observatory, was in the *Field Guide* (1964 edition), where there was the bald statement, 'Smaller than common Swift, which it resembles except for almost square tail and *white rump*'. Since there was no reference to the very conspicuous white throat patch and I knew that there were other white-rumped swifts to be taken into account, I immediately sent my notes to Major R. F. Ruttledge so that comparison with the literature could be made. In the event, however, certain identification as a Little Swift (this name superseding 'White-rumped Swift' for *A. affinis*) came through discussion with I. J. Ferguson-Lees when I returned to England a fortnight later. The field-characters of this and similar species have since been described in detail by Ferguson-Lees (1967).

My field notes and sketches have been examined by M. P. L. Fogden, Dr C. H. Fry and D. I. M. Wallace (all of whom are familiar with this and other white-rumped species of swift), in addition to I. J. Ferguson-Lees, Major R. F. Ruttledge, and the Records Committee of the British Ornithologists' Union. Despite the present debate over the identity of the white-rumped swifts nesting in southern Spain (Allen and Brudenell-Bruce, 1967; Benson *et al.*, 1968; Milstein, 1968; Fry and Elgood, 1968), all are agreed that the Cape Clear Island bird was *A. affinis*. The three species of swifts with white rumps most likely to occur in Britain and Ireland are the Little Swift, the White-rumped Swift *A. caffer* and the Horus Swift *A. horus*. The latter two are both larger than *affinis* and both have very deeply forked tails (often appearing pointed in flight), whereas *affinis* has a short square-ended tail. The broad white rump patch is also diagnostic of *affinis*. All these differences have been dealt with in more detail by Ferguson-Lees (1967) and by Fry and Elgood (1968).

work through the local Recorder, you can send the record to the editor of the journal *British Birds*, at the editorial address (Macmillan Journals Ltd, 4 Little Essex St, London WC2R 3LF), and he will then treat it in a similar way. When a bird has been seen in Britain for the first time, the full notes are later published in *British Birds*; it is valuable to look up some notes in back numbers of this journal in order to appreciate how full such notes can be, and how clear a picture of the bird they can give. If you are not able to subscribe to the journal yourself, your local library should certainly be able to let you see copies in the reference section.

What to write

Often these full-length field notes will have three sections, and only the middle one of these three will have been written in the field. These sections are: firstly, an introduction, in which the observer states where he was, what time of day it was, what other birds he had been watching, and then where he noticed the rare bird, what drew his attention to it, and how long he watched it for; who else watched it with him, and why he lost sight of it in the end. The second section will then be the complete description of the bird, feather tract by feather tract, including size, shape, posture and behaviour. And the last section will be written after the event, in which the observer explains why he thinks it was the species he has named, why it was not any other more common species, and what knowledge the observer has to draw on which leads him to this conclusion (such as having seen this species before while on holiday abroad).

Naturally it is vital that any observer who is going to write notes of this quality must be properly prepared in the field with notebook and pencil, and must be very familiar with the names of all the feather tracts. It is useful to practise writing such notes before you have a genuine rare bird to write about. On a warm summer day when it is comfortable to keep still for a long time watching a Spotted Flycatcher in a park or a Song Thrush on a lawn, why not practise some full-length notes on these? It is also a good idea to have a check-list handy of the points you ought to make notes on in the field. The check-list might look like this:

size	crown	secondaries
type of bird	nape	coverts
striking points	mantle	stance
where it was	rump	gait
what it was doing	tail	calls
main colour areas	chin	manner of flight
eye stripes	throat	other birds seen with it
wing bars	lores	observers
tail feathers	breast	range
leg colour	belly	light
beak colour	under tail coverts	binoculars used
forehead	primaries	how long observed

any other points, e.g. speculum in the case of ducks, whether feet were webbed, etc.

Since the bird you are writing notes about is alive, it will probably not be kind enough to allow you to notice all these points in the right order. Then again, you may get two or three different views of some of these points, and the colours may not seem the same every time you see them. So long as you preserve the original notes in a safe place, it is quite legitimate to sort out the order of the notes later on. You may finish up with a note that says 'When the tail was first seen, it seemed to be slightly notched, but this was not seen again, and seen from below it definitely appeared square-ended.' A note of this sort can be very valuable, because it reveals how the bird has closed and spread its tail; as was shown on page 50, details of this kind can often be crucial in clinching an identification.

Which birds need full-length notes

Full field notes will be needed for many subspecies of common birds seen on passage, as well as for the extreme rarities; and the rule must always be, that if one is in any doubt, full field notes should be written. It is no use at all writing the plumage description later on. Notes are likely to be needed therefore if you see a White Wagtail inland in England, perhaps for a Scandinavian Lesser Black-backed Gull or even a Greater Black-backed Gull in some inland counties, for a Marsh Warbler in most areas or a Red-backed Shrike almost anywhere in Britain. Even common birds can be 'rare' if they are in very unusual places or seen at very unusual dates. I had to write full-length field notes on Carrion Crows seen in south-west Ireland (where all the crows usually seen are Hooded Crows), and I would write them on a Swallow if I had the good luck to see one in January. It is most of all in knowing what notes are wanted, and what detail would be appreciated, that previous contact with the local Recorder can be so valuable. Requirements for each species are bound to vary from county to county.

Some observers become rarity hunters. They draw up lists of the number of species they have seen in a month, a year, or a county, and they concentrate on adding new species to these lists rather than looking more closely at the birds that they have already seen around them. Many of these rarity hunters become very expert ornithologists, with an amazing precision in their identification. But you must be warned that the checking and the vetting of field notes can be a disappointing experience. However gently, tactfully and scientifically it is done, if a Committee (or a local Recorder) after due consideration has to reject your record, it is hard not to be bitterly disappointed. If you try hard to find rare birds you are more likely to finish up with a number of rejections among your acceptances.

On the other hand there is no point in running away from field notes and the vetting Committees. If you are indeed looking at a Crested Lark, it is no good saying 'It can't be; it doesn't happen to me, I don't see rare birds!' To put a bird that is really a Crested Lark down as a Skylark is just as inaccurate, and just as undesirable, as the opposite fault of trying to make every House Sparrow a Spanish Sparrow.

2   Counting Birds

No one knows which is the commonest bird in Britain. No one knows how many birds there are in Britain. No one knows how many millions of birds come into the country to spend the winter here, or how many come to breed here.

Nevertheless, great progress has been made in recent years in counting birds.

The next two chapters describe various breeding-season counts, and mention a few ways of watching population levels at other seasons also.

Counting birds is incredibly difficult. They move, they migrate, they hide, they swarm in swirling flocks that defy the expert, or crouch in wild open spaces where it is difficult to go. Some birds like town life, others shun the company of man; some birds stay inland all their lives, others spend most of their lives at sea or in the air. It is not really surprising that there is no firm knowledge of which is the commonest bird in the whole of Britain, or that it is only in recent years that we have gained any proper knowledge of the numbers of our breeding seabirds. As I write this on a cold October morning, there is no one who can say, even within a few million, how many birds are in Britain today, or what proportion of the ones that are here are birds that were born here, or how many have just arrived across the North Sea to enjoy our rather milder winter. There is now a count made every summer of a few of our breeding birds, and this tells us a little of the bird population in April, May and June. But there is no count at all, absolutely no count, of winter numbers.

The Common Birds Census

The Common Birds Census (strictly speaking, the Breeding
Season Census of Birds) is a census of the birds on a number of
fixed areas made year after year. In 1972 there were 152 areas
censused; 88 of these were farmland areas and 64 were woodland. The farmland areas are fairly large; at an average of 73
hectares (181 acres), they are each the size of an ordinary mixed
farm with about ten fields, and each of these farmland areas may
have eight kilometres of hedge. The observer (or team of
observers) that has chosen to make this census covers the area at
least eight times during the breeding season, and records every
bird he sees in the area. Details of the maps, the codes and the
techniques are given in the next chapter. The results are analysed
by the full-time experts at the British Trust for Ornithology
(B.T.O.) headquarters, and from the results of all the areas a
population index is obtained. This shows how the overall

population level in these sample areas changes from year to year. It is thought that there are so many areas being counted, and that the areas are so scattered and varied, that these results are probably a fair indication of the changes in the overall numbers over the whole country each year. But they never tell us what those numbers actually are.

The examples of results given on pp. 62–3 by courtesy of the B.T.O., show just how difficult it is to monitor the population levels. Colossal changes may occur from one year to another, and many of these changes may have happened outside Britain. While the census can show the results of these changes, it cannot tell us where or when they happened. The crash of Whitethroat numbers, for example, may well have been the result of a spring drought in equatorial Africa. The rise in Wren numbers may be the result of high survival during the series of mild winters; a hard winter kills off perhaps three-quarters of all the Wrens in Britain.

The results of the census are very good considering the

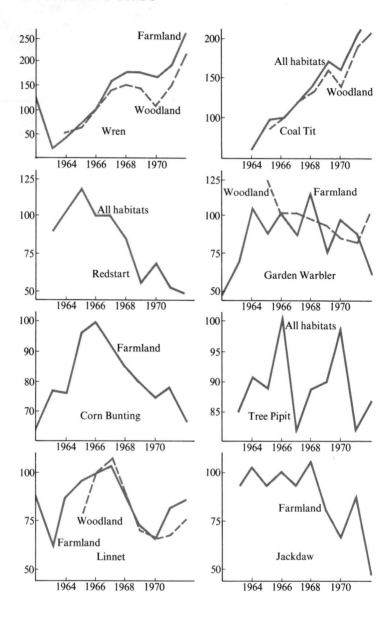

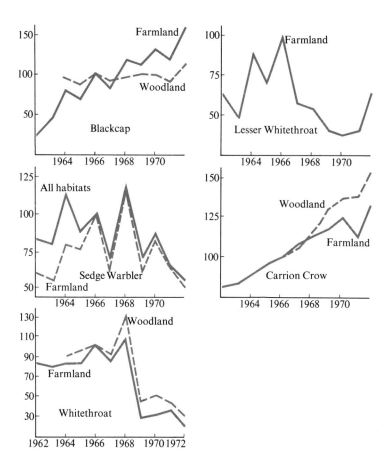

Changes in the breeding population levels shown by the Common Birds Census. The breeding population levels of the year are expressed relative to 1966, which equals 100. Note how some levels have been halved in the period and others increased

difficulties involved, but one has to be alert to the intrinsic inaccuracies. A report by S. M. Taylor in *Bird Study* has shown that the technique works much better for some species than for others, but it also works better at some population levels than at others. Evidence of a territory is usually based on the observation of *singing* males; but on a farmland area I censused for several years after the hard winter of 1962–3, there were so few Blackbirds in the first years that the males did not need to sing in order to hold a territory. As the population level rose, the size of the territories had to be reduced, and the males had to sing a lot to defend them. A huge increase in song rates was quite out of proportion to the increase in sightings. The census technique, in other words, could underestimate low populations.

Waterways survey

A variation on the farmland or woodland census is the waterways survey. Observers select a few kilometres along a river or canal, and census all the birds breeding along it. The technique is the same as for the Common Birds Census, but you are likely to finish with rather different species – you are obviously more likely to get Moorhens and Kingfishers and less likely to get owls or woodpeckers.

Counting colonial birds

Some other birds are best counted by other methods. In the case of colonial birds – birds which live in colonies – counting the nests is likely to be the most accurate and obvious method. Herons in Britain have been counted in this way every year since 1928 and the population graph obtained is one of the best studies of the numbers of birds made anywhere in the world. Other birds that can be counted well in this way, if you can be sure to find all the colonies, include Rooks, Sand Martins, and seabirds.

Counting very local birds

There are other birds where close study of a map will reveal likely places to look, and if you check all of these you can be reasonably sure you have checked the entire local population. Swallows are very much birds of barns and outbuildings, and a careful search around these places should enable you to count how many are flying in and out. Getting landowners' permission to enter and count the nests is obviously the best way to do this, but a rough estimate can be made from public rights of way by watching the swallows feeding in the vicinity of their nests.

Nightjars are birds of heathland, young plantations or sandy foreshores, and these areas are rather local (particularly in the southern half of England). A systematic search of such areas at dusk on summer evenings is likely to enable you to make a good survey. We have made such surveys with Nightjars in Berkshire and Corn Crakes on Cape Clear. Linear studies can be made of birds like Dippers, Kingfishers and Common Sandpipers, that are confined to fast-flowing streams – so long as care is taken to look a little way up each side stream flowing in.

Counting seabirds

Seabirds can sometimes be counted with ease: Razorbills and Guillemots may be lined up in rows in the small and medium colonies, allowing almost perfect precision over the number nesting. Shags and Cormorants make large messy nests, and can also be counted fairly easily. Puffins, petrels and Shearwaters, however, being burrow nesters, are much more difficult to search out, and accurate counts of these are unlikely to be possible for a beginner. Problems can also arise in counting large colonies of gulls, terns, or Gannets. With many of these it may be necessary to count how many there are within a specified small area, and work out from this how many there are likely to be in the whole colony.

The Seabird Group have recently mounted the first national

census of our breeding seabirds, and Dr Bill Bourne has published some results in *B.T.O. News* (December 1973), as well as a much more detailed report in the book mentioned on page 187. It seems that the three commonest breeding species in the British Isles are the Guillemot, Puffin and Kittiwake, with around half a

Atlas maps of Stock Dove (opposite) and Tree Sparrow (below) showing the areas of the British Isles where these two species breed (big dots) or are present in the breeding season (small dots). Each dot represents a record obtained within a ten-kilometre square of the national grid

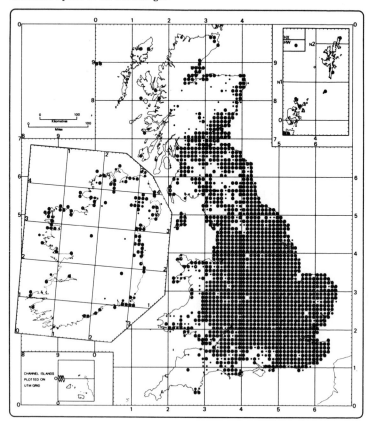

million birds each. Our scarcer breeding species include Black Guillemot, Cormorant, Great Skua, Roseate Tern, Little Tern, Arctic Skua and Leach's Petrel – in each case there are probably between one thousand and ten thousand pairs breeding each year.

Distribution

I have been concerned so far with the *number* of birds nesting in a particular area. But there is also the question of which parts of

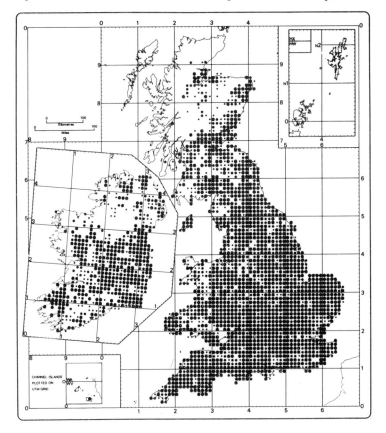

the country each species nests in. Here again, detailed knowledge is fairly recent. A national survey has recently been completed by the B.T.O. and the Irish Wildbird Conservancy, mapping whether or not a species nests at all in each ten-kilometre square of the British Isles. In many cases the distribution of our birds proved to be different from what had been thought previously. The two maps shown on pp. 66–7, by courtesy of the B.T.O., give more details about the distribution of these two species than is suggested in most reference books.

Counts outside the breeding season

A few species are counted at other times of year. A detailed survey of the waders around our shores is being made every winter, because a large proportion of all Europe's waders winters here. Industrial and reclamation schemes exist for every major estuary in Britain, and if most of these are carried out there will be no winter feeding area left for many species. These surveys have shown that the commonest wader around our coasts is the Dunlin with up to 500,000 birds present; other species abundant, at least in the passage season, are Knot (250,000) and Oystercatcher (200,000). Full details have not yet been published, but a report is being prepared. Another regular winter count is that of wildfowl, which is made on the first weekend of every month throughout the winter. The British wildfowl counts began in 1948, and now similar counts are made at the same date across most of Europe and in Russia. Grand totals of somewhere around one and a half million wildfowl are counted, of which nearly half are to be found wintering in the British Isles. The results of these counts have been published in *Wildfowl*, the journal of the Wildfowl Trust.

Periodic surveys are made of the wintering numbers of Starlings and gulls, particularly those going to roosts. In a similar way, special surveys are mounted for rare species when an 'irruption' occurs, and abnormal numbers of Waxwings, Bearded Tits or Crossbills winter in Britain.

These special surveys are very valuable and interesting, but they do not amount to a good winter survey of inland birds. The grid square survey described in the next chapter is something that can be done fairly easily to give a general impression of numbers and distribution in a substantial area, and many species can be counted in roosts during the winter months. Alternatively, actual daily counts of the birds in a fixed area can be interesting, but it is not wise to draw too many conclusions from the counts of just one or two areas.

3 Counting Techniques

Census techniques

If you would like to enrol to do a census for the B.T.O. you should write to the Populations Section there for details. Before you begin on this, you should be able to identify all the common species accurately by sight and many of them by call and song. You should also be in a position to plan to do the census over several seasons: a count from just one year is no use to the B.T.O. survey. You will need to do at least eight counts each season – it is better if you can manage ten counts each year. How long the count will take varies with the area, but it will usually last between four and eight hours a time. This is a lot to take on. The results are fascinating and absorbing and fully justify the work, but you should only enlist with the B.T.O. scheme if you feel sure you can do this much.

Perhaps, however, you have in mind a smaller area which you would like to census for your own interest. Common Birds Census code symbols and techniques should be used, together with census analysis methods. Here is how it is done.

Choose the area

If you have some choice of area to do your census on, there are a few points that are worth bearing in mind.

From the point of view of the B.T.O.'s census, any area chosen should be fairly typical of the surrounding countryside. You will need to have clearly defined borders, and if possible you should choose your area in such a way that any special feeding places, or particularly rich nesting areas, are well inside it, and the outer parts of your area are not particularly rich in bird life. It follows of course that you will need to do a certain amount of bird watching in the district before you can decide what would make a good census area – unless you have decided to count the birds on a particular area because they belong to a particular company, person, or corporation. Naturally, areas with a good variety of habitats will have a greater variety of birds, but for the purpose of the B.T.O.'s census farmland or woodland are preferred.

Area maps

As soon as you have checked that you can have permission to wander all around the area, obtain maps of the scale 1 : 2500 for the whole area concerned from the local Ordnance Survey agent. If you show the agent on a standard 1 : 50,000 O.S. map exactly where the area is, he will be able to order the right maps for you. (In a few simple areas you may be able to map it yourself, but an accurate scale map is essential for this work.) In other cases you may be able to scale up from the cheaper 1 : 25,000 series.

Trace the O.S. map and go round the area with the tracing. There may be changes since the O.S. map was drawn, e.g. hedges removed or new buildings erected. Plot these. It is also invaluable to put in obvious landmarks, such as isolated tall trees, or trees standing much higher than the hedges, stand pipes, stiles, hydrants, even fence posts or places where the farmer parks a trailer regularly. If possible, add detailed habitat notes on all hedges (e.g. 'hawthorn cut to 2 m, with ditch', or 'hawthorn and bramble, no ditch'), and record which fields are ploughed each year and which are permanent pasture. Do a neat copy of this map at home, and then have about fifty copies run off by some inexpensive method. Stencils are cheap to use if you have access to them (for example, in a school). Commercial concerns can make copies but these will prove expensive.

Official B.T.O. symbols for Common Birds Census work

Ⓑ   singing male Blackbird

B̲   Blackbird giving alarm call

B   material   Seen with nest material in beak

B   food   Blackbird seen with food in beak

⸜Ḇ Ḇ⸝⟶   Two males fighting (movement shown by arrow)

B∗   Blackbird nest

B or Bσ or B♀ or B juv   Sight record of Blackbird with details where possible

Ⓑ----Ⓑ   Different Blackbirds in song at the same time

Bσ---- Bσ   Different male Blackbirds in view at the same time

Ⓑ——Ⓑ   Singing bird seen to take up a new position

Ⓑ—?—Ⓑ   Thought to be same Blackbird, but not certain

B∗----B∗   Nests in use at same time and therefore belonging to different pairs

For colonial birds, use symbol and put number in brackets, eg. LI (8)

Visit maps

From the beginning of April, visit the census area at regular intervals (once a week if possible) and make a complete count of every bird seen, marking each one on the map. A list of symbols and the standard abbreviations for different species are shown above. It is best to use pencils for field-work (ball point pens quickly dry up out of doors), and you will need a clip board to rest the maps on. (It is likely that when you have the maps duplicated the large map of the area will be cut into pages of A4 or similar size, which are more convenient in the field anyway.) You will also need a list of the symbols until you have learnt them. Locate each bird carefully; there will be plenty of room for

LIST OF CENSUS SYMBOLS

MA	Mallard	SL	Swallow	BC	Blackcap
K	Kestrel	HM	House Martin	GW	Garden Warbler
RL	Red-legged Partridge	SM	Sand Martin	WH	Whitethroat
PH	Pheasant	C	Carrion Crow	WW	Willow Warbler
P	Common Partridge	JD	Jackdaw	CC	Chiffchaff
MH	Moorhen	MG	Magpie	GC	Goldcrest
L	Lapwing	J	Jay	SF	Spotted Flycatcher
SN	Snipe	GT	Great Tit	D	Dunnock
WK	Woodcock	BT	Blue Tit	MP	Meadow Pipit
CD	Collared Dove	CT	Coal Tit	TP	Tree Pipit
WP	Woodpigeon	MT	Marsh Tit	PW	Pied Wagtail
TD	Turtle Dove	WT	Willow Tit	YW	Yellow Wagtail
CK	Cuckoo	LT	Long-tailed Tit	SG	Starling
LO	Little Owl	TC	Treecreeper	GR	Greenfinch
TO	Tawny Owl	WR	Wren	GO	Goldfinch
SI	Swift	M	Mistle Thrush	LI	Linnet
KF	Kingfisher	ST	Song Thrush	LR	Lesser Redpoll
G	Green Woodpecker	B	Blackbird	BF	Bullfinch
GS	Great Spotted	R	Robin	CH	Chaffinch
	Woodpecker	GH	Grasshopper	Y	Yellowhammer
LS	Lesser Spotted		Warbler	CB	Corn Bunting
	Woodpecker	RW	Reed Warbler	RB	Reed Bunting
S	Skylark	SW	Sedge Warbler	TS	Tree Sparrow

all you see, as shown in the illustration on p. 74. Make sure you cover the whole area. Record the date, time of beginning and finishing, and the weather. File the map carefully.

Repeat this for each visit, using a new map each time. Three visit maps are shown on pp. 74–6. If you manage a visit every week you will finish up with at least twelve maps by the end of June. There is usually little point continuing census work later than this.

At the end of the season you will want to go on to the next stage, so that you can estimate what the population of territorial males in your area actually was. This means that you must prepare species maps.

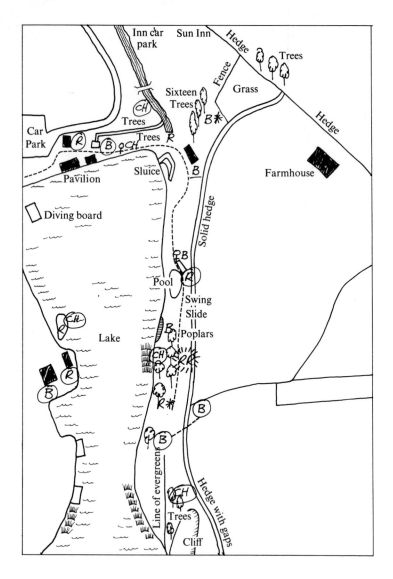

First visit: 7.30 a.m. to 10.15 a.m., 2 April. Warm, cloudy

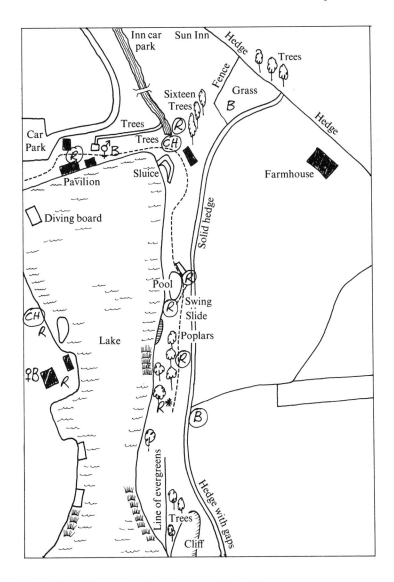

Second visit: 7.15 a.m. to 9.45 a.m., 9 April. Cold, windy

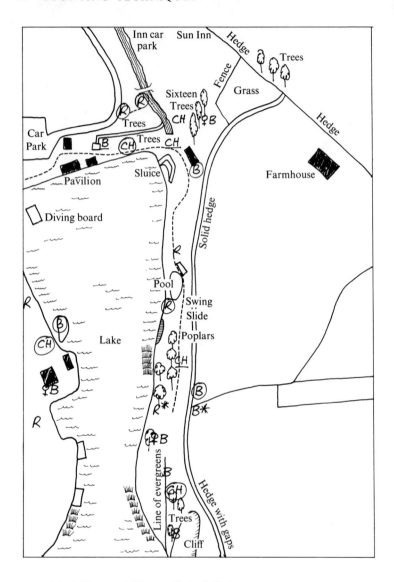

Third visit: 2.30 p.m. to 5.00 p.m., 20 April. Hot, sunny

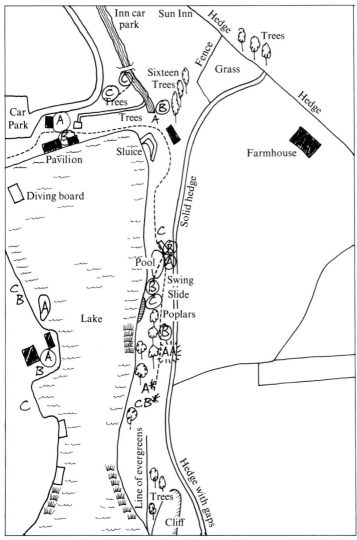

A species map (Robin) of the same area

Species maps

Take a new clean map of the area and label it (for example) ROBIN. Collect all your visit maps, put them in date order, and label the visits A, B, C, D, etc., starting with the earliest and finishing with H, J, K, or L, as appropriate, for the last. Pick up the map for the first visit, find all entries for Robin (e.g., R, R̲, Ⓡ, R* and so on), and copy these in the correct place on the species map with the *visit letter standing in place of* the species letter (e.g., A, A̲, Ⓐ or A* and so on. Repeat for each visit (giving you B, B̲, Ⓑ and B* for Robins on the second visit, and C, C̲, Ⓒ and C* for Robins on the third visit, and so on). An example of a species map is given on p.77. When you have completed this, decide the limits of each territory. The rules in the table on p. 79 will help you draw territorial lines. Add up the territories, counting edge birds as half.

Repeat for all other species holding territory. As an economy, less well distributed species can 'share' maps, using, for example, a red pen for Redstarts, and a black one for Blackcaps, on the same map.

Census results

The following year you will begin to see changes in the population. Can you explain them? Are they in line with the national trends? Year by year the progress of an area becomes more absorbing. The table on p. 80 gives the number of territories recorded by the Nottingham club over four seasons at one part of Attenborough Gravel Pit. At the beginning of the survey the area concerned had only just been excavated, and the growth of willows and reeds had just begun. By the end of the survey shown in the table, these wetland plants had covered the area quite thickly. This is the sort of area that can make a very rewarding local study, although for the national survey farmland or certain types of woodland are preferred.

Minimum evidence required to establish a territory depending on the number of visits made

	Six or fewer visits (an inadequate total for a good census)	Seven, eight, or nine visits	Ten or more visits
Best	Occupied nest. No other information necessary.	Occupied nest. No other information necessary.	Occupied nest. No other information necessary.
Second best	Two song registrations fairly close together.	Two song registrations fairly close together and one other sighting nearby.	Three song registrations fairly close together.
Next best	One song registration and registration of territorial fighting, or courtship display, or bird carrying food on at least one other occasion; or signs of nest, e.g. newly fledged young or broken eggshell.	Two song registrations and one other similar record, or one song and two other similar records.	Two song registrations and one other similar record, or one song and two other similar records.
Barely adequate	One song registration but seen in immediate vicinity on almost every visit.	One song registration or evidence of territorial behaviour but seen in vicinity on at least six visits.	Two song registrations or evidence of territorial behaviour but seen in vicinity on at least six visits.
Inadequate (do not record a territory)	No song or other territorial behaviour.	One or no song registrations or other evidence of territorial behaviour, unless seen in vicinity at least six times.	One or no song registrations or evidence of territorial behaviour.

This table has been prepared by the author as a 'do-it-yourself' guide to analysis and is not a copy of any guide used at B.T.O. headquarters.

Census results from western end of Attenborough Gravel Pit (Notts.) 1967–70

Species	Territories held in			
	1967	1968	1969	1970
Great Crested Grebe	?	?	5	6
Tufted Duck	0	?	4	?
Canada Goose	0	0	0	1
Mute Swan	3	0	4	2
Moorhen	?	?	4	4
Coot	5	?	c.13	?
Skylark	5	?	7	13
Carrion Crow	2	?	1	6
Blue Tit	1	0	1	1
Wren	3	?	1	1
Song Thrush	0	?	3	2
Blackbird	3	?	9	4
Sedge/Reed Warbler	7	?	4	21
Willow Warbler	0	?	2	3
Dunnock	2	?	4	7
Meadow Pipit	1	?	4	5
Starling	4	?	1	1
Greenfinch	1	?	2	1
Linnet	6	?	8	1
Reed Bunting	7	?	19	20
Tree Sparrow	2	?	2	0
Total territories	50	?	86*	99†

* excluding Sand Martin.
† excluding Coot, Tufted Duck and Mallard.

Birds in colonies

Counting of birds in colonies needs to be done at the height of the breeding season, although it may be necessary to make some preliminary counts. Rooks, for example, are best counted just before the buds burst at the tops of the trees, but if you are covering a substantial area and cannot be sure of getting round all the rookeries on the right week-end it will be necessary to count a few a week or two in advance; usually by early April most of the nests will have been built and counts will be at any rate 95 per cent complete. In many areas Rooks nest in substantial rookeries and for once large-scale maps are not necessary; a list of all known Rookeries, with six-figure grid references from the 1 : 50,000 O.S. map, and a total for occupied nests will be quite sufficient. On the other hand in parts of Wiltshire, for example, Rooks are distributed along the tall trees of many hedgerows, and at times one has to plot the nests hedgerow by hedgerow.

Results of surveys by the Nottingham club show that, for some reason not known, Rooks were gradually moving away from the Trent valley and moving further up on to the Wolds for nesting sites.

House and Sand Martins

House Martins have such restricted nesting sites that they can be counted by a systematic search along the streets, recording the door numbers of the houses where they are nesting. This method naturally does not allow one to record any that are nesting at the backs of houses, but a straight comparison from one year to another should not be seriously inaccurate. House Martins are dependent on supplies of mud for building their nests, and this means that they usually nest within a few hundred metres of a stream or pond. It also means that the date of the peak of their nesting season varies a great deal from year to year; it may be delayed for several weeks by a drought, finishing with a spurt of intense activity around every puddle after a summer thunderstorm, as they all collect building material. A satisfactory House Martin survey therefore needs to be maintained throughout the summer months, and it is normal for young birds of later broods to be still in the nest in mid October.

Sand Martins nest in colonies in any suitable cliff face they can burrow into – perhaps only a few feet high, or perhaps at quite inaccessible heights. It is fairly easy to count how many holes there are in such a colony (except where large entrance holes divide into two or more burrows further in), but it is not so easy to be sure how many of the holes are in active use. Cobwebs and other tell-tale signs may sometimes indicate that a hole is not in use, but in many cases it may be necessary to watch the colony from a sufficient distance for a while, observing carefully with binoculars which holes are being used. Peak activity tends to occur just before dark, as the parents roost in the nest holes in the breeding season.

Wildfowl and waders

The Wildfowl Trust run a wildfowl count every year. This has been established so long that there are regular watchers recruited for most waders in Britain, but if you would like to know whether you will be useful as an observer, write to the Organizer of Wildfowl Counts at the Wildfowl Trust, Slimbridge, Glos. The B.T.O.'s wader census is now complete except for some continuation studies and occasional special inquiries, and here again regular observers are available for supplying most of the information that is needed at this time. Inland observers often find these species difficult to identify accurately at a distance, but observers who spend a lot of time at the coast are naturally much more competent. If you would like to do some wader counting, you could inquire from the B.T.O. whether any more help is needed in your area.

Grid square survey

A grid square survey is a survey you can arrange yourself, and is an easy way of watching the distribution of species in your home area, as well as assessing the numbers.

The way to begin is to take the ordinary O.S. map, and trace a road map of your area, with the one-kilometre grid lines. Have this map duplicated – you will need a large number of copies. Each month, use one map for each species you are interested in, and record on the map whether you have seen the species in the area. If you have been into a particular grid square but not seen the species at all, put an X. If you have been there but not seen more than 10 birds of this species at any one time, put a 1. If you have seen up to 100 birds at a time put a 2, and up to 1000 at a time put a 3; for any larger numbers put a 4. Leave blank any squares not visited, although you should aim to cover the same squares each month if you can. It will probably be possible to cover about 20 squares a month on your own, or more if your friends help you.

Examples of the proportion of squares found to have a given species (in any numbers), as recorded in south-west Nottinghamshire, are shown on pp. 84–5 for Kestrels and Pied Wagtails. Both these species were well distributed and present in all months; we had therefore not realized before doing the grid square survey how much Kestrels were birds of autumn passage and Pied Wagtails were winter visitors (probably from further north in England).

Grid Square Survey Results (Notts)
% of squares visited where Pied Wagtails were seen

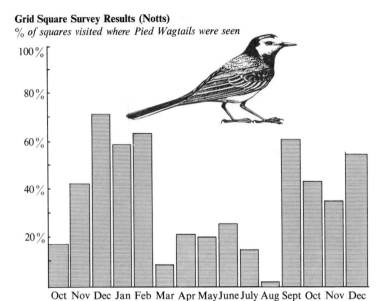

Daily counts

In an area near your home that you know well you may be able to count all the birds almost every day and most of the year round. If you can manage to do this at about the same time each day the results will be interesting. It is a good idea to enter them up in columns on loose-leaf paper so that you can keep inter-leaving more sheets. You can then turn the pages and read off the numbers of any one species simply by following along the line. If you write the species names on the left-hand side of the back of the first sheet and cut all the other sheets down, to make them narrower, you will not have to keep on writing out the names. It is important of course to begin with a list of all the

Grid Square Survey Results (Notts)
% of squares visited where Kestrels were seen

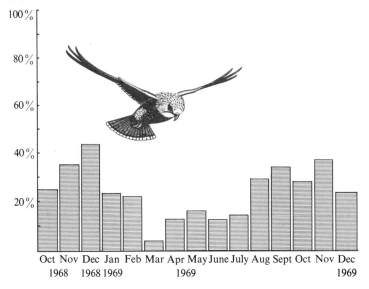

species you expect to see in the area during a year. This will surely include all of the sixty species in chapter 1 of this book, and probably another twenty or so species according to the type of area it is. (If you include birds flying over, and I think for this count you should, almost any area, even in a town, can produce over fifty species during prolonged study.) Any unexpected species will have to be added at the end out of Wetmore Order, or inserted on the blank lines. This will not matter so long as your list was full enough to begin with. Otherwise you may have to re-copy it – a long job!

A list of this sort, which is not as strict as a census list, can include birds seen or heard flying over, but it is a good idea to list the ones that seem to be on long-distance movement

September 1975

	23	24	25	26	27	28	29	30	1	2	3	4	5	6
House Martin	6	5	8	6	8	12	10	12	22	8	35	6	8	6
Carrion Crow	2	2		2	3			2	1			1		2
Rook	15			12							18			
Jackdaw			1					1						
Magpie	1	2				1	3	1						
Great Tit	1		1	1		2	1				2	1		
Blue Tit	2	2	1		2	3		1	3	1		3	1	2
Marsh Tit	1	1	1					1						
Longtailed Tit							12							
Wren	1	1	1	2	1	2	1	1	1	1	2	1	1	1
Mistle Thrush		3		2	2	3				1				1
Fieldfare														
Song Thrush	1	1	2	1	1	2	↲	1	1	2	2	2	1	1
Redwing					←16						←23			
Blackbird	4	5	4	6	4	5	6	4	6	5	5	4	4	6
Robin	1	2	1	1	1	1	1	1			1	1	1	1
Blackcap	1		1-2							1		2		

October 1975

	7	8	9	10	11	12	13	14	15	16	17	18
House Martin	12	14	12	14	28	26	30	25	30	20	15	14
Carrion Crow	1	2	1		3		1	2	1	2	1	
Rook			21		12	4	2					
Jackdaw	2				1				3			
Magpie	1	2		2	2		1	1	1	2		
Great Tit	2	1			2	1	6	3	2	1		4
Blue Tit	2	1		3	2	1	3	9	6	9	3	4
Marsh Tit												
Longtailed Tit					8							
Wren	1	1	2	1	1	1	2	1		1	1	2
Mistle Thrush	3		1	2		3	2		1	3		
Fieldfare	↙6				↙50	↓20			←10			
Song Thrush	1	2	1	1	2	1	1	2	2	1	1	1
Redwing	150				↓100	↓80	↙20					
Blackbird	10	12	10	13	12	10	11	13	12	11	12	13
Robin		1		1	1	1			2	1	1	1
Blackcap	2-3	1-2	1									

separately – for example, a separate count and an arrow indicating the compass direction of flight. Flights to and from roosts can be recognized partly by the time of day, and partly by the regularity with which you see them. These are best listed entirely separately. If you are on the flight line for a large roost these numbers will swamp all your other counts. Any unidentified birds seen flying over are probably best forgotten altogether.

One other small problem remains to be discussed – what happens when you keep seeing just one bird of a species and you do not know if it is the same individual or not? The best solution to this is to record the lowest and highest possible numbers, e.g. 1–5, 3–8. This problem is less serious with bigger numbers; it matters most when it could be just one or two birds constantly reappearing.

(Opposite) Daily count records kept on loose-leaf paper. The illustration below shows the reverse of the right-hand page above

4 The Importance of Finding Nests

Since the success of nests holds the key to the population levels of the future, it is important to study them. Finding them and recording them all takes a lot of skill.

The next two chapters outline ways of recording what is needed with the minimum of disturbance for the bird. Suggestions are also made for encouraging birds to nest.

Finding nests – obvious ones or difficult ones – is an exciting business. It's fun to find a clutch of eggs clustered together, and fascinating to study their progress: to see the mother bird sitting day after day, to see the new-born young that seem so shapeless and ugly, and to see how quickly they develop into attractive young birds crowded together round the rim of the nest, gazing at the world outside. Part of the excitement is in finding something that has been hidden, part of it is the sheer beauty of the eggs, and part of it the universal feeling of pleasure in seeing young living things.

So I wonder why small children so often destroy nests by taking the eggs? Are they unable to look ahead to the day when the young birds will hatch out? Or is it that they think only about the new-born young, ugly, lumpy and ungainly, without being able to visualize the same birds a couple of weeks later, well-fledged, beady-eyed, perky and bright?

The law passed in 1954 and adjusted in 1967 is quite specific and very good. All birds, nests and eggs are protected, except a few species that damage farming very seriously and 'sporting' birds. Common birds are protected in the same way that rare species are protected. The full details are fairly complicated, because some species (such as Bullfinch) are protected in most of the country but not in certain counties where large quantities of fruit are grown (because Bullfinches take flower buds in spring). The Royal Society for the Protection of Birds has produced a little booklet called *Wild Birds and the Law* which includes all the lists of specially protected and unprotected species.

One point of law which I think is worth dwelling on is that eggs are protected even when the nest has been deserted. If you think about this, it has to be so, because otherwise anyone found with an egg collection could always claim that all the eggs had been deserted before they were taken. Some people do not realize that a bird will leave eggs cold in the nest until she has laid the last egg of the clutch (so that when she does start incubating, all the young can develop together and hatch at the same time). These people think that the eggs have been deserted and it is all right to take them. To explain that they are not deserted, and that you cannot take them even if they are, makes a big difference.

Good seasons and bad seasons

There are good seasons and bad seasons for each species. These variations can be considerable, and are the chief reason why it is important that close study is made of thousands of nests of common birds every year. Obviously the weather plays a huge part. One year many young tits died in the nestboxes in our survey areas because when they were about a week old bad weather brought heavy rain continuously from dawn to dusk; the parents were unable to find food, and the young died of starvation and cold while the parents were out searching. Another year some young Blackbirds in our area died because of the drought; the heavy clay soil baked like brick in the hot sun, the parents were unable to find enough moist food, the young birds turned a strange yellow ochre colour, and only a few survived. Every species is at the mercy of the weather, although different features trouble different species.

There are many more subtle variations than this. The annual variation in the number of eggs laid, for example, is much less closely linked to the weather. Of course it is true that while she is laying eggs the mother bird needs quantities of good food, but nature has arranged it that she can lay eggs and deprive her own body of nourishment if necessary. Variations in clutch size often seem to be linked to something much less immediate than the food available when the eggs are being laid. There may be a distinct connection between clutch size and the overall population of a species. If the population is high, clutches will be smaller. Alternatively there may be a connection between clutch size and the amount of food that will later be available for the young when they hatch. Research on tits has hinted at this possibility, but it is not yet clear how the parents can foresee how much food will be available and control the number of eggs they lay. We can assume that they do not 'think' about it, but that the hormones in their bodies carry out the control for them.

But nothing is simple. The number of eggs laid may indeed vary with population level, but it also varies with the locality, habitat, and the part of the country the bird is living in; this shows, once again, how impossible it is to decide much from a purely local survey. Blue Tits in oak woods are likely to lay twice as many eggs as those in gardens; but in one particular locality there could be a variation in one of these habitats and not in the other. Again, passerine birds in the North of England or Scotland are likely to lay more eggs than those in southern counties.

National results

When a nest has been studied carefully, no matter how common the bird may be, the details are of interest to the B.T.O. The national Nest Record Scheme collects information from observers in every part of the country, and the analysis leads to conclusions about variations in clutch size, and, much more important, the number of young produced each year. A rapid fall in the number of young produced would, of course, be investigated, and might be related to the use of some form of agricultural spray, or a change in farming practice, as has occurred with Partridges and Quails. (The modern methods of agriculture involve cultivating land that was previously left as rough grazing, and also putting large machines into fields to harvest the corn and to plough in the stubble much earlier in the season than it was possible to harvest the crop in the days of simple binders and threshers. This has led to a complicated series of changes in the insect life of cornfields, which has been made worse by weedkillers eliminating the weeds that many insects breed on; and this, in turn, has reduced the food available for Partridges, and probably also Quails, to feed to their young, leading to a steady decline in numbers.) If it were practicable for anything to be done to reverse the trend, the B.T.O. would contact the Ministry of Agriculture, or the Home Secretary, as appropriate. Naturally a national survey is needed to establish points of importance; the disasters I mentioned on pp. 89–90 were confined to one locality. The overall effect on the numbers of the species concerned may have been slight, and any empty territories in the area could easily have been filled by birds moving in from more successful areas. There are times, however, when the disaster is not local but national, and the national survey can show how bad this is.

In recent years the B.T.O. has published detailed analyses of the nest records of the following species: Buzzard, Sparrowhawk, Merlin, Lapwing, Ringed plover, Woodcock, Stock Dove, Woodpigeon, Turtle Dove, Cuckoo, Corvidae,

Long-tailed Tit, Treecreeper, Mistle Thrush, Song Thrush, Ring Ouzel, Blackbird, Spotted Flycatcher, Meadow Pipit, Grey Wagtail, Greenfinch, Chaffinch, Yellowhammer and Tree Sparrow. These reports have covered annual and local variations of date and clutch size, typical nest sites, and success rates; and they depend entirely on the reports of local observers.

So by watching carefully even the common nests near your home, and sending in the reports to the B.T.O., you can contribute valuable information to a fascinating and important national survey. Obviously there is no other way of getting the information about breeding success within Britain, and it is only with this information that we can make a proper study of our birds' year.

5 Field-Work on Recording Nests

Nest record cards

If you want to make nest records, either for your own use, or for sending in to the B.T.O. later on, it is important to record the right information in the right way.

The things that are really important to know about any nest are:

what species made it
where it was built
how many eggs were laid
the date the clutch was completed
date(s) when the young hatched
how many young survived until a few days before departure
when the young left the nest, or when the nest was destroyed.

You do not have to record all these points, however – although, of course, a report containing all of them is the best possible. As long as you have managed to record one point accurately, it will be useful and will be welcome at B.T.O. headquarters. So even if you only find a nest because you see the young leaving it, for example, the record is well worth making.

Record it all in six visits

The ideal nest record would be one in which the observer obtained all the above information in six visits, only five of them

OBSERVER DORCAN SCHOOL O.S. (HUMPHREY M. DOBINSON)					SPECIES		YEAR 19 75	B.T.O.F
					CHAFFINCH			

NO. of EGGS or YOUNG at each visit.				Record here stage of building; if bird sitting; if eggs warm; age of young; ring nos. etc.	COUNTY	If this record is entered on ATLAS CARD put ✓ in box	Offic Use O
DATE		G.M.T.	EGGS	YNG.		WILTSHIRE		D
Day	Month							
4	May	08	3	0	♀ flew off	LOCALITY (place-name) Grid Ref		C
8	May	10	?	?	♀ sitting			
16	May	11	5	0		CHISELDON 184 804		H
22	May	10	0	5		ALTITUDE above sea level .... 420 ...ft.		
25	May	16	0	5	Ringed	HABITAT Delete those inapplicable:- RURAL/SUBURBAN/URBAN		F
30	May	15	0	5	well fledged			
1	June	11	0	0		Steep valley with rough grass and trees.		

NEST SITE

Hawthorn bush.

NEST RECORD CARD

BRITISH TRUST FOR ORNITHOLOGY, BEECH GROVE, TRING, HERTS.

Please consult instruction leaflet for method of completing cards,
advice on visiting nests, and what observations are most useful.

A few reminders:-
1. Clubs and schools should give their name as well as the observer's.
2. Use one card for each nesting attempt, even if a nest is used twice.
3. Record all counts of eggs or young, even if number is unchanged. To avoid mistakes, please write the month, e.g. 5 April, not 5/4.
4. Accurate counts of eggs and young are important, but if there is uncertainty put a ✓, or put brackets round the probable number.
5. Do not forget to record any eggs remaining unhatched.
6. Final visit: please enter date and nest-contents overleaf, and indicate your findings under "Outcome of Nest" below. The central space below can be used for further visits and/or notes.
7. RECORD ONLY WHAT YOU OBSERVE. PLEASE MAKE NO GUESSES

5 young ringed, numbers JN88208-12.

OUTCOME OF NEST

If you have positive evidence that the young left safely, or of failure, please put a cross (☒) in the appropriate box or boxes below. Otherwise mark the appropriate 'Outcome Unknown' box.

OUTCOME UNKNOWN
{ Because evidence for or against success is inconclusive ☐
{ Because observations on nest were not continued ☐

EVIDENCE FOR SUCCESS
Young: capable of leaving nest when last seen ☐
Young: seen leaving naturally ☐ left when approached ☐
Young: seen and/or heard near nest ☐
Parent bird(s): giving alarm calls ☐ carrying food ✓
In nest: hatched shells ☐ feather scales ☐ droppings ✓
Any other evidence:

EVIDENCE FOR FAILURE
Nest: empty ☐ damaged ☐ fallen ☐ flooded ☐ removed ☐
Eggs: damaged ☐ deserted ☐ all infertile or addled ☐
Young: all dead, uninjured ☐ all dead, 1 or more injured ☐
Any other evidence (e.g. type of weather causing failure,
species of predator if seen, etc.):—

ght above ground or cliff-base 6

Both sides of a Nest Record Card supplied by the B.T.O. These cards can be obtained from the B.T.O. office for making fair copies of notes of nests recorded during the season

being while the nest was in use. Extra visits will add no information of value (if there are three eggs on 20 April and five on 22 April, it is a pretty safe guess there were four on 21 April; and even if there were not it does not really matter). The more visits you make, the greater the danger that the bird will desert or the nest be robbed by a predator seeing you go in, or following your tracks. Some careful planning of dates after your first visit will help to reduce the number of other visits necessary.

What sort of nest is it?

Of course the best way to decide what sort of bird built the nest is to see the parent on it, and if there is any doubt about the species you must watch to see this. Apart from seeing the parents, the best clue to species can often be found from the size, shape, place and material used for the nest, rather than from the eggs, because eggs can vary a lot even when laid by only one bird. While the first eggs are being left cold, you are most unlikely to see the parent around, and the chance of desertion is greatest: take a quick look, record what you can, and get away, covering your tracks carefully behind you. Later on you may find the mother incubating. If she sits tight so you cannot see the eggs, leave her alone and go without the information about how many eggs there are. When the parents are feeding, you are unlikely to have to wait more than a few minutes to see one of them, as long as you stand away from the nest and let them go in.

Where is it built?

Information about where the nest is built can be important to studies of habitat preference. The height above the ground should be estimated carefully, and note made of the type of bush, tree, outbuilding or hole it is built in.

Nest visit planner

Species	Common nest site	Main materials	Peak season	Likely number of eggs	Likely period of incubation (days)	Likely period before fledging (days)
Great Crested Grebe	edge of lake	old reeds	May	3-4	28	Nidifugous*
Cormorant	cliff	seaweed	end April	3-4	30	50
Heron	tall tree	sticks	April	3-5	26	56
Tufted Duck	under bush	grass, feathers	end May	7-8	24	Nidifugous
Mallard	ground	feathers	April	10-12	28	Nidifugous
Canada Goose	ground	feathers	April	5-6	28	Nidifugous
Mute Swan	water's edge	reeds, sticks	April	5-7	35	Nidifugous
Buzzard	tree	big sticks	end April	2	35	45
Kestrel	old crow's nest	none	end April	4-5	28	28
Common Partridge	ground	feathers	May	8-20	24	Nidifugous
Pheasant	under branches	feathers	May	12	27	Nidifugous
Moorhen	edge of stream	reeds	April/May	5-12	21	Nidifugous
Coot	edge of lake	reeds	April/May	6-9	21	Nidifugous
Oystercatcher	among rocks	none	May	3	25	Nidifugous
Lapwing	fields	grass	April	4	26	35
Curlew	rough grass	grass	April/May	4	28	Nidifugous
Snipe	marsh	grass	April	4	19	Nidifugous
Lesser Black-backed Gull	bracken	grass	May	3	28	Nidifugous
Herring Gull	cliff top	grass	May	3	28	Nidifugous
Common Gull	cliff	grass	May	2-3	24	Nidifugous
Black-headed Gull	boggy ground	water weeds	May	3	23	Nidifugous
Woodpigeon	hedge	twigs	July	2	16	21
Collared Dove	tree	twigs	June	2	14	19
Cuckoo	nest of Meadow Pipit or Dunnock	—	May/June	12?	11	21
Tawny Owl	big hole in tree	none	March/April	2-4	28	35
Kingfisher†	hole in river bank	none	May	6-7	19	23
Great Spotted Woodpecker	hole in trunk	none	May	4-7	12	22

Species	Location	Material	Month	Clutch		
Swallow	inside barn	mud	May/June	4–5	14	20
House Martin	the outside of houses	mud	June–October	4–5	14	19
Carrion Crow	big branches	twigs	April	4–5	19	31
Rook	small branches	twigs	end March	3–5	18	29
Jackdaw	hole in tree, old chimney	grass	April/May	4–6	17	30
Magpie	thick hedge	ball of twigs	April	5–6	21	25
Great Tit	hole in tree	moss	April	gardens, 7 woods, 12	14	19
Blue Tit	hole in tree	moss	April	gardens, 7 woods, 12	14	19
Long-tailed Tit	hedge, shrub	ball of moss	April	8–12	15	15
Wren	brushwood	grass	May	5–6	14	16
Mistle Thrush	thick bare branch	polythene, grass	April/May	4	13	14
Song Thrush	hedge	mud-lined	April/May	4–5	12	13
Blackbird	hedge	grass-lined	April/May	5	12	13
Robin	fallen leaves	leaves, hair	April/May	5–6	14	14
Dunnock	thick hedge	grass, hair	April/May	4–5	12	12
Sedge Warbler	reeds	stalks	May	5–6	13	13
Whitethroat	brambles	dead grass	May	4–5	11	10
Blackcap	brambles	roots	May	5	11	11
Willow Warbler	hedge bottom	moss	May	6–7	13	13
Chiffchaff	brambles	moss	May	6	13	14
Spotted Flycatcher	against tree trunk	moss	June	4–5	13	14
Meadow Pipit	long grass	dry grass	April/May	4–5	13	13
Pied Wagtail	steep bank	moss	May	5	13	14
Starling	hole in tree	grass, feathers	April	5–6	12	21
Greenfinch	evergreen shrub	twigs, hair	May	4–6	13	13
Goldfinch	apple tree	hair	May	5–6	12	13
Linnet	hawthorn scrub	bents, hair	May	4–6	12	14
Bullfinch	hawthorn hedge	twigs	April/May	4–5	12	14
Chaffinch	high branch	moss	April	4–5	13	13
Yellowhammer	hedge bottom	stalks	April/May	3–4	13	12
Reed Bunting	marshy tussocks	old grass	May	4–5	13	10
House Sparrow	inside loft	long grass, feathers	April/May	3–5	11	15

* Nidifugous means the young can leave the nest soon after hatching.

† Kingfishers are one of the species on Schedule One of the Bird Protection Act, which means they must not be disturbed at the nest without a licence from the Natural Environment Research Council.

Not so easy to count

It is best not to touch eggs because they are broken very easily – their shells are usually much thinner than the shells of hens' eggs. Count how many there are carefully. Large clutches can be very difficult to count accurately because of the way they are arranged in the nest, and in addition, some birds cover some or all the eggs when they leave. If it is necessary to disturb the covering, it should be done very delicately and the covering replaced when the eggs have been counted. The table on pp. 96–7 tells you roughly how many eggs are usually laid, so you can work out when to go to the nest next in the hope of seeing a full clutch. (Most birds lay one egg a day, usually soon after dawn.)

Guess when they will hatch

A similar calculation can tell you when to go to the nest expecting to see newly hatched young. Remember the mother sits on the nest most of the day when the young have just been hatched. It is very difficult indeed to count newly hatched young because they are not yet strong enough to hold their heads up, they are still blind and almost naked, and lie on top of each other. At this stage however an exact count is not important; what is important is whether they have hatched.

Guess when they will fly

It is best to play safe for the next visit, and go two or three days before you expect the young to leave. It is very important to go up quietly because at this age the young will often 'explode' from the nest if they are frightened or disturbed. It is quite wrong to attempt to touch them, even if you cannot be sure how many there are.

Did they get away?

A final check a few days later is likely to provide a clue on whether the young all left successfully. If the nest was raided, its lining will probably have been torn; if the young left successfully, there may be one or two droppings left in the base of the nest, but otherwise it should be clear. There may be scales from the newly grown feathers left in the nest.

There are usually clear signs to show when a nest has been raided by some wild animal rather than by egg thieves. Eggs that have hatched are usually chipped in a neat ring, and the membrane inside the shell is slightly stained. Eggs that have been broken by a predator are more often than not split right open, and the membrane inside is completely clean (if it has not got some egg spilt on it). Most natural predators damage the lining of nests. There are so many natural predators that the majority of nest failures are caused by them and not by egg thieves.

Work out some results

The more records you can get, the more results you will be able to obtain from your work. Analysis of records from a relatively small area (twenty or thirty kilometres across) can be both meaningful and interesting. The smallness of the area can easily make up for the fact that not nearly so many nests are being analysed as in a national survey. In this way, our analysis of nests recorded by members of our club showed big differences from year to year in the clutch size of Blackbirds nesting in the area, which dropped from an average of 4·00 in 1969 to an average of only 3·29 in 1970. There were clear differences between one wood and another in the dates and clutch sizes of Blue Tit and Great Tit nests. While comparisons from one year to the next are particularly interesting, it is also interesting to see within one season what differences there are in clutch size and success between first and second broods or between different species. Do some species seem to be considerably more successful than others? Do they lay as many eggs? Do you think you are as good at finding their nests as at finding the nests of less successful species?

Nestboxes in woods

It is quite simple to put up many nestboxes and thus be fairly sure of finding a lot of nests very easily! If you set about this in the right way it need not be a very expensive undertaking.

First, of course, you must find a wood where the boxes can be set up. Unfortunately a lot of people are curious to see what is in a box, so it is best to find a private wood, or to put the boxes well out of view if you are thinking of using a wood where the public will go. When you ask the owner for permission, ask also how the boxes should be fixed to the trees. Many foresters prefer that the box is wired to the tree rather than being nailed on, as the nail spoils the timber.

In thick woodland, boxes can be set quite close together. You can mix the sizes and shapes of the boxes, so as not to have two identical ones close together. We have often had two nests within ten metres of each other. It is certainly profitable to put up boxes at distances of about twenty metres apart. Vary the height and the direction of the hole faces.

Building the boxes

It is often possible to obtain large quantities of rough wood free or almost free. Many industrial concerns, warehouses and supermarkets have a large number of broken pallets or wooden boxes, and these are often burnt. If you can find someone with a van or a truck to help you take the big load away, this rough wood can be taken apart and sorted for use. Much of it will be unsuitable but there should be enough for your purposes. It will not be top quality wood but, although much of it will be thinner and poorer than the wood recommended in many books for building nest-boxes, it will do. The Nottingham club had over 300 boxes in the local woods and we were not aware of any nest failures as a result of poor wood. It would have been out of the question to have built more than thirty boxes with good wood, and we had plenty of evidence that there was a shortage of natural nest sites in all the woods we used, so that our boxes helped to boost the breeding population of tits and Tree Sparrows considerably. My own view is therefore that it is better to make more boxes from thinner wood, than to be such a perfectionist that only a few boxes are made.

Mass-production methods have much to recommend them. The diagram below shows how to cut out pieces from one board if it is long enough. Pile up a big stack of backs and fronts, then of sides. (If some boards are thicker than others, use the thick ones for backs and fronts and bottoms, and the thin ones for the sides and the tops.) Drill holes in the fronts with a brace and bit if possible, but if this is not possible, a square hole cut in one top corner is remarkably successful. Nail (or screw) together backs, fronts and sides; cut floors to fit, then saw lids to fit with a little overlap at the front.

All sorts of ways of hinging lids have been suggested in books. Some go rusty, others are difficult to make, others are expensive. We have found that a cheap quick way is to fix bits of useless

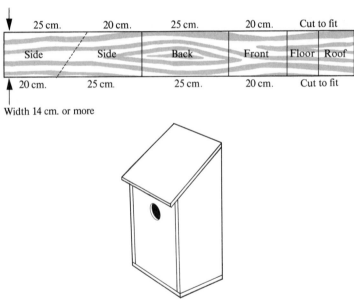

25 cm.	20 cm.	25 cm.	20 cm.	Cut to fit	
Side	Side	Back	Front	Floor	Roof
20 cm.	25 cm.	25 cm.	20 cm.	Cut to fit	

Width 14 cm. or more

Cutting wood to make a nestbox

wood inside the lid to make a tight fit, and then to loop a bit of wire over the top of the box to stop the wind (or squirrels) lifting it off.

Do not be too good a carpenter. Rough wood is more natural than smooth planed wood, and gives the young birds more to grip on when they scramble up the sides. A few small gaps in the floor will be covered over with nest material but will be useful for drainage. Birds do not measure up their homes with set squares and plumb lines and will not know whether the corners are perfect right angles or not. On the other hand, *do* make sure that the bottom is fixed safely; that the lid will not come off accidentally; that you put the box the right way on the trunk so that rain will not drain in; and that there are no bad cracks in the front or the sides.

All these principles of manufacture will apply to boxes made for tits, other hole nesters, Robins, Blackbirds, Kestrels, owls and so on. Details of the sizes and shapes for other species are well described in the B.T.O. guide to nestboxes. We have tried several of them, but have not yet had anything other than Squirrels and Starlings in them. But we keep on trying.

Mapping the boxes

When the nestboxes are ready, you will need a good large-scale map of the wood, its paths and landmarks. Boxes can be put up at any time during winter months (we have had nests in boxes put up on 3 May, although March ought usually to be considered the deadline) – but whatever the date is, the leaves will be off the trees when you put the boxes up. One day in May you will revisit the familiar wood to find everything changed; and you will not be able to find some of your own boxes! Broad leaves can open very suddenly and transform the look of paths, gaps and openings. A good map is essential.

Boxes will need to be numbered. It is a help if the numbers can follow the order in which you will check them each time, but this is not important so long as they are well mapped. It is easy to get in a muddle and use the same number twice – keep very careful records. Record what sort of tree you put it on (if you don't know what type it is, at least record its size), how high the box is, and which way it faces. Remember to fix the box so you can see into the top later on – it is easy to fix an empty box and then find later that it is just too high to see into. Secure the box firmly so it cannot fall off even in a gale. If you are wiring it, use 14 gauge ('Elephant') wire, and twist the ends tight with pliers. It can take a long time putting the boxes up.

When checking the boxes, a record sheet like the one shown here, or a notebook ruled in this way, is invaluable. At the end of the season, an interesting trip cleaning out old nests may reveal winter nests of mice where the birds had been!

Dorcan Ornithological Society

NEST BOX RECORDS

DATE: June 2nd   PLACE: BRAYDON   OBSERVER(S): HHD

Box No	SPECIES	E	Y	NOTES	Box No	SPECIES	E	Y	NOTES
1	Blue Tit	?	?	BIRD oN					
2	Blue Tit	12	0						
3	Great Tit	?	6	About 4 days old					
4	—	-	-	Empty					
5	MISSING								
6	Tree Sparrow	4	0						
7	Blue Tit	1	9	Ringed JN88481-9					
13	—	-	-	Empty					
14	-	-	-	Empty					
15	—	8	-	A few bits of straw					
18	Blue Tit	13	0						
21	Blue Tit	?	6+	Just hatched					
22	Marsh Tit	8	0	Bird heard nearby					
23	—	-	-	Empty					
24	Great Tit	8?	2	Just hatching					

Nestboxes in gardens

It is possible to have several birds nesting in almost any garden, if a variety of boxes are put up; even the bare rectangular patch found behind so many houses is likely to be attractive for nesting Blue Tits, Great Tits, Starlings and House Sparrows, and there is a reasonable chance of a more exciting bird nesting there also – a House Martin perhaps, or a Wren. Privet, lonicera and other evergreen hedges around such gardens are good nesting places for birds like Dunnocks, while garden sheds can attract Blackbirds and Song Thrushes, which might use a box put out for them there. Ideas for suitable boxes can be found in the B.T.O. Field Guide *Nestboxes*, and, despite the unlikely title, in T. Soper and R. Gillmor's *The New Bird Table Book*.

Nests in winter

Nests in use can be found from February (Mistle Thrush) to November (Woodpigeon, Town Pigeon), with even an occasional one in December and January, but the main interest of the winter is to find all the nests you missed in the summer. A large-scale map is useful, and on this you can mark all the old nests found once the leaves are off the trees. You can learn a great deal about the favourite locations of Chaffinches, Linnets, or *Sylvia* warblers (Blackcap, Garden Warbler, Whitethroat and Lesser Whitethroat) that escaped detection. You are less likely to come across, or recognize, any of the nests built on the ground of course. The best book for the identification of nests is *Nesting Birds, Eggs and Fledglings* by W. Reade and E. Hosking. Although old nests can be collected for analysis and display, they are difficult to take out without damage, and are messy and bulky to store. (They can have quite a large collection of living creatures in them too!) On the other hand, interesting measurements of the nest can be made, and the range within a species, and the contrast with other species, discovered by analysis. This can be done without pulling the nest out at all.

6 Migration: The Fascinations

If Man ever had the ability, possessed by birds, to know his exact position, he has lost it now. The way birds can move around, and the way they can retrace their steps, is one of the most fascinating things about them. But their journeys are often hazardous, and many do not have a successful outcome.

Studying migration is important to our overall understanding of the birds' lives and their changing numbers.

The next three chapters discuss some of the more intriguing aspects of this topic, and suggest ways of studying it either at home, or on a journey of your own.

A solitary young Willow Warbler, weighing less than ten grammes, will battle its way for thousands of kilometres to Africa, fend for itself there in the subtropics all winter, and return safely to the same wood that it was born in. How does it cope with finding its way, with the strong winds high up in the air, with crossing the sea and the desert? How does it manage to time its journeys so that there should be enough food in all the countries where it wants to eat? And how long does it take the bird to carry out this incredible journey?

The marvels and mysteries of migration are endless, and after years of intensive study, the answers to many questions are still very vague and incomplete – often they raise as many questions as they solve.

Navigation, for example. It is now moderately well established that most of our small birds migrate by night and navigate chiefly by the stars. It is also clear that the position where the sun sets is likely to help greatly towards fixing a bearing. But:

● How do the birds know which stars to navigate by?

● How good is their sight?

● Do all species have good eyesight, or are some able to see only the bright stars while others can see fainter ones?

● Since stars appear to move across the sky during the night, how do birds have such an exact sense of time that they can use the sun and stars for navigation at all? (For the precision of navigation that we observe in birds their time sense must be right within much less than an hour.)

● How do their brains allow for the variation in the observed position of the stars that they see which comes about through the passage of time combined with their own movement over hundreds of kilometres?

● What happens when the stars are clouded over, or fade with the dawn?

● Does the Earth's magnetic field help them to hold their course? Many birds take routes that are 'Great Circles'. These are the shortest routes to take, but they involve bearings quite different from those found with a compass. A wader migrating from England to eastern Siberia, for example, is changing its compass bearing all the time.

Even for our Willow Warbler, it may be that the answers to all these questions depend on whether it is a male or a female, a northern or a southern breeder, a young bird or a veteran of many journeys, and whether the season is a stormy or a sunny one.

The astonishing and exciting thing about migration study is the fact that many of the most important things to be found out can still be solved by a patient observer without a car, a ringing licence, or any technical equipment.

Dates of main arrivals

In my opinion the greatest priority for home-based observations of migration is to establish not the dates of the first and last birds of each species, but the dates of the main arrivals and departures, especially of the females. If we are truly concerned about conservation, it is inadequate to consider any conservation efforts we might make purely in the light of the needs of the showy pioneer males which are the ones many observers eagerly record for the 'arrival' date. It could be, for example, that in a development area one particular tall tree is always favoured as a song perch by the first Chiffchaff to arrive each spring, but a much less conspicuous and less attractive cluster of trees is the main feeding area of the female. The male could find another song perch, but the female cannot find another feeding area at that date in May. And what date is that anyway? We have only the haziest idea.

The home-based observer can monitor details of the dates and success of migration that may often be highly significant for the species concerned. The members of my club made careful daily records of their observations in south-west Nottinghamshire. In May 1969 our club report carried an item: 'Where have all the Whitethroats gone?' Gradually, as the summer went on, it became clear that the lack of Whitethroats was not just a local phenomenon as we had expected it to be; the national population as monitored by the Common Birds Census had fallen by about 77 per cent, and falls had occurred all across Europe. A report published in 1974 looks into this change and relates it to years of drought on the southern edge of the Sahara where Whitethroats winter, and where they must find enough food in spring to fatten up for the long journey across the desert to the north. The 3000 kilometres across the desert are a much bigger hazard to a bird than the relatively narrow strips of water they must cross, such as the Mediterranean, the English Channel, the Irish Sea or the North Sea, none of which normally involve more than 800 kilometres of open water.

Other movements

But migration is not simply the arrival and departure of our summer migrants. There is migration of some sort occurring on more than half the nights of every year, and other long-distance movements on almost every night. There are few species where the whole population remains in the same area all the time. Marsh Tits and Willow Tits, and perhaps Little Owls and Jackdaws, must be almost the only truly sedentary British birds.

The three main groups of migrants are the summer visitors, the winter visitors, and the passage birds (e.g., waders and sea-birds); but besides these, there are the migrations of a part only of the population, often, but not always, the young birds. Many of our finches, along with Meadow Pipits and Pied Wagtails, are involved in movements of this type. All of these are migration as strictly defined – a regular seasonal movement from one locality to another *and back again*. In addition to these migrations many other sorts of movement occur.

There are the dramatic irruptions and eruptions when large numbers of birds (e.g., Waxwings) move into or out of an area – something that may happen only once every few years. These movements are different from migration because it is not clear whether the birds all go back where they came from; and the areas they go to may differ from time to time. Some of our common birds, like Blue Tits and Dunnocks, are known to erupt occasionally.

Post-breeding dispersal and 'shunting'

There is also the post-breeding dispersal of the young birds of our 'resident' species, much of it occurring in a listless and piecemeal way during the doldrum months of July and August. But daily surveys, as described in the next chapter, also reveal big movements in October; big, that is, in terms of numbers – we do not know about distance. Nor do we know what these movements are, how regular they are, or what triggers them off. For want of a better word, this type of movement can be called 'shunting'. Shunting may be very significant for the species concerned, but at present it is almost unnoticed and completely unexplained. The home-based amateur has a huge field to work on here.

Calls in the night

It is surprising how many birds you can hear flying over at night, particularly in the first few hours after dark. The peak time to hear such calls inland is in October, when the majority of the calls are of Blackbirds and other members of the thrush family, but it is possible to hear some calls in many different months of the year. Early July can be a good time for hearing several species of waders, even far inland.

The extent of the thrush-type calls in autumn and winter is astonishing, and it is possible that a proportion of them are made by birds simply flying around for a bit after dark, perhaps

'keeping in practice' on their night star map and orientation, in case they have to make a long-distance movement during a spell of hard winter weather. Or can all these birds be really on passage, night after night, right into December? Some systematic observation of the conditions under which such calls are heard, and the species involved, would be very illuminating.

Bird observatories

A visit to a bird observatory will give an opportunity to see some very different aspects of migration. There are about twenty bird observatories around the coasts of Britain. Each one is independent, and the organization varies, but they all have many things in common. Each one has been set up to allow amateur ornithologists to study migration, each one keeps meticulous daily records of all observations and ringing, and each one offers simple cheap accommodation. Most have a paid warden in charge, but some cannot afford this. None of them exist to make a profit and most operate on a shoe-string budget all the time.

Administration is always in the hands of unpaid enthusiasts who often work very long hours for the observatory concerned.

The observer who wants to watch, to record and to work will be more than welcome at any British or Irish bird observatory. Details of how to write and book a place are given on page 128.

7 Migration: Getting On with Recording It

Migration into and out of a locality

As the previous chapter has shown, there are different types of migration and other movements, and therefore naturally there are different ways for an amateur to study it. The suggestions made here are for ways which will tell a single observer, or preferably a small group of observers scattered over ten or twenty kilometres, something meaningful about the movements of birds in their areas. Since migration is a long-distance journey, usually undertaken by many thousands of birds, results of national significance can only be obtained by national surveys, and these are outside the scope of this book. Yet it is astonishing how few County Bird Recorders know when the main arrivals of summer migrants occurred in their counties, less still the main departures, or the dates of the big autumn invasions of Blackbirds, Woodpigeons, Lapwings and Starlings. The methods mentioned in this chapter should help with all of these.

The most rewarding method of studying arrivals and departures is by a series of daily counts in known areas. The basis of this approach is that, since most small birds migrate at night on a broad front, they are likely to appear, rather randomly distributed, over a wide area on the morning after their arrival. Similarly, since they depart from widely scattered locations, they are likely to disappear from similar areas at this time. If counts are made of all the birds present in an area every day, changes in the numbers can be compared with changes in the numbers present in other similar areas, and when the same changes are found in a number of areas on the same day it indicates that migration has occurred.

For this method to be valid, certain rules must apply:

1. The area in which counting takes place must be exactly the same every day.
2. The count in any one area should be done by the same person every day. (One person may of course count several areas in a day.)
3. The count in each particular area should be done at the same time each day.
4. There must be counts made in several quite different areas.
5. The same route, in the same direction, should be taken every day.

What sort of area will do?

Anywhere with a good variety of birds can be studied for a migration count. You might choose:

school grounds
grounds of a work place
town park
a piece of waste ground
allotment gardens
or a country lane.

The size of some areas may be much greater than other areas, and the time taken to make the count may be as little as ten minutes or as much as an hour. For this sort of count (which is not a census) it is a good idea to include birds identified on short flights over the area, and it is also all right to include birds on trees or buildings just outside the property you are walking round so long as you always count all birds seen on them.

The area does not need to be mapped, and therefore its shape may be most irregular. What is important is that you make your own rules and stick to them. It is no good deciding one day 'I'd love to be able to put that Cuckoo on my list and it's only just outside so I may as well include it; I'm sure it's on migration.'

The other study areas in the district may have quite different habitats, and be quite a different shape. This will not matter so long as each one is studied carefully, and all the counts are made in the morning. In spring and autumn the best counting time is usually between half past seven and half past nine, but counts made up until lunch time can be used. It is unwise to include any counts made after lunch, because the birds have been disturbed so much, and may have moved on or gone into hiding.

Observers should note the weather, and if anything has happened which might upset the count (a cat-fight for example!) it might be best to ignore the figures obtained that day.

Working out the results

Finding out what migration has taken place is not just a matter of adding up all the birds seen each day. The table of imaginary counts for Willow Warblers on p. 116 will be used for explaining two ways you cannot use, and then the way that ought to be adopted.

You will get misleading results if you just add up the total number of birds seen each day, because unfortunately neither Tom nor Jackie made counts on 20 April, and as it happens their areas had more Willow Warblers in them than all the other areas put together. All the other areas except John's showed an arrival of Willow Warblers then, and if Tom and Jackie had made their counts they might well have seen thirty birds between them; but without their counts the block graph of daily numbers shows only a very small peak that day (see top graph, p. 118).

Nor can you overcome this by taking the average number of birds per area – for the same fundamental reason: some areas are better than others for a particular species (see middle graph, p. 118).

Table of imaginary counts for Willow Warbler

Observer	Type of area	April										
		14	15	16	17	18	19	20	21	22	23	24
Tom	woodland	3	3	3	6	4	4	—	—	—	(+1)* 10	(+1) 14
Dick	allotments	0	0	0	0	0	0	(+1) 1	0	0	0	0
Harry	large garden	1	1	—	1	—	1	(+2) 3	—	0	1	2
Susan	pony's field	0	0	0	0	0	0	(+1) 1	0	1	1	1
Sheila	town park	1	1	0	1	1	1	(+4) 6	3	5	6	5
Sally	footpath past a field	1	1	1	—	1	1	(+2) 3	1	1	—	1
Jackie	country walk	4	4	5	6	4	3	—	—	(+2) 12	10	13
John	several small gardens	0	—	0	—	0	0	0	0	—	0	0
Jeffrey	school grounds	0	—	0	0	0	0	(+2) 2	—	—	0	2
Total areas counted		9	7	8	7	8	9	7	5	6	8	9
Total birds seen		10	10	9	14	10	10	16	4	19	28	38
AVERAGE SEEN PER AREA		1·1	1·4	1·1	2·0	1·25	1·1	2·3	0·8	3·2	3·5	4·2
Total weighted value of increases		—	—	—	—	—	0	12	0	2	1	1
Average weighted value per area counted		—	—	—	—	—	0	1·7	0	0·3	0·1	0·1

* Figures in brackets refer to weighted values (see below).

The way that will work: weighted values

The best way of sorting out the results is complicated, and requires a good set of records; but this is the only way which allows fully for the fact that the 'best' Willow Warbler areas were not counted on 20 April.

Look through the counts made in each area each day. Numbers are always fluctuating, and you must decide what the normal fluctuation for each area is. To do this, take the first five days after a new area is begun to establish the levels; from then on you can analyse each area daily until there is a long break, when again you will need five days to establish the normal pattern. Assuming all these areas began counts for the first time on 14 April, Sheila's area usually has no birds or just one, but Sally's and Harry's seem to have one bird regularly; Tom's and Jackie's areas have numbers varying from three to six.

After the first five days, if the number of birds seen has gone up or down outside the normal fluctuation, give the change a *weighted value* depending on how big it is. The table on p. 119 sets out all the weighted values. If 20 Willow Warblers are seen in an area that usually has 16 Willow Warblers a day, this is the same proportional increase as if 10 are seen in an area that usually has 8. In both cases the rise is up to one and a quarter times the earlier figure, and so both increases just qualify for the smallest weighted value increase of $+1$. If the area that had had 16 suddenly produced 40 birds, this would be an increase by two and a half times, and so would have a weighted value of $+2$. (It would also be $+2$ if the count had risen to 47 or 55 or 79 – it rises to $+3$ when the increase is five-fold.)

Next add up all the weighted values for the increases; divide by the number of areas open each day; and your results give a reasonably reliable indication of the arrival of Willow Warblers into the district.

The same table can be used to record *decreases*, which should be given negative weighted values $(-1, -2)$. Never cancel positive results against negative results – you are trying to record migration, not overall population figures, and if six birds leave some areas and six arrive in others, this is a busy spell of migration and should show as a peak of increases and decreases.

Total of Willow Warblers seen in all areas—a misleading graph

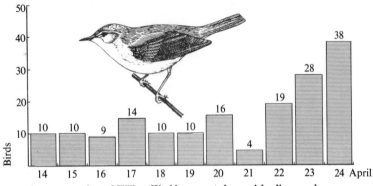

Average number of Willow Warblers counted—a misleading graph

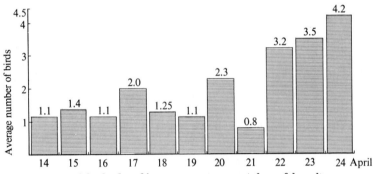

Average weighted value of increases per area counted—useful results

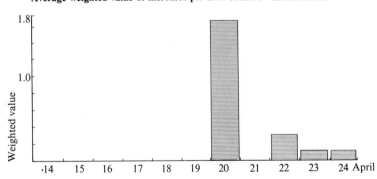

Weighted values of increases and decreases

Factor of change Weighted value	1·25 1	2·5 2	5·0 3	10·0 4	20·0 5	50·0 6	100 or more 7
Pre-increase maximum, or new ebb figure	New maximum, or figure from which numbers have fallen						
0	1	2	4	8	16	40	80
1	2	3	5	10	20	50	100
2	3	5	10	20	40	100	200
3	4	8	15	30	60	150	300
4	5	10	20	40	80	200	400
5	7	13	25	50	100	250	500
6	8	15	30	60	120	300	600
7	9	18	35	70	140	350	700
8	10	20	40	80	160	400	800
9	12	23	45	90	180	450	900
10	13	25	50	100	200	500	1000
11	14	28	55	110	220	550	
12	15	30	60	120	240	600	
13	16	33	65	130	260	650	
14	18	35	70	140	280	700	
15	19	37	75	150	300	750	
16	20	40	80	160	320	800	
17	21	43	85	170	340	850	
18	23	45	90	180	360	900	
19	24	48	95	190	380	950	
20	25	50	100	200	400	1000	

What do the results mean?

Results obtained from either of these methods tell us how much variation there was in the number of birds seen in the study areas that day. It does not follow that this variation was migration, and there is no way of *proving* if it was migration or not. It is safest therefore to give these movements a name like 'shunting' or 'shifting', and then to interpret them by using other information. For example:

The Willow Warbler increase on 20 April (and the small level of shunting on 22, 23 and 24 April) comes at a time when spring migration can be expected, and the numbers remained higher. It is reasonable to suppose that this was true immigration.

In the same way, decreases of Swallows from the end of August onwards are likely to be emigration (birds leaving the country).

A peak of Whitethroats can be expected in early July. This is a time when 'post-breeding dispersal' occurs. No one yet knows how far this is random 'shunting' and how far it is the beginning of the return passage – we do not know if the birds are in fact heading south, or wandering in all directions.

A peak of Dunnocks can be expected in October. This is totally unexplained. Although 'irruptions' have been known (that means arrivals from abroad when population levels are high there), there is no evidence from ringing recoveries to suggest anything like enough birds move long distances to explain these 'shunting' records. Why do the results suddenly show a peak like this?

A peak of Starlings can be expected at the end of May. This is when all the young leave the nests and is not migration at all.

A peak of Lapwings can be expected in June. This is when the young birds can fly and parties begin to move to new feeding areas. There is a lot of work to be done to explain why the birds want to reach new areas.

A peak of Blackbirds, Woodpigeons and Starlings can be expected in October. Huge numbers arrive across the North Sea at that time, and much of what is recorded in the study areas is probably true immigration.

Hard weather in winter may produce big changes. Some of these represent a change from one feeding area to another, others are longer-distance movements.

It is only general knowledge, common sense, and the application of all other relevant information that can guide the interpretation of results.

Weather maps help

When you think the movements you have recorded may be long-distance ones, it can be very instructive to look at weather maps. There is plenty of evidence from many years of migration watching and radar observations on birds to show that:

● most species of birds usually set off just after dark and fly through the night;

● they only set off when the sky is fairly clear and there is little wind or a following wind. They seem to use the stars to guide them;

● they fly above fog and mist, except towards the end of their journey or when lost;

● they do not like to fly through warm fronts with thick cloud and rain;

● they can be moved somewhat off course by wind;

● they usually drop down low if they enter thick cloud;

● headwinds slow them down and following winds speed them up; their speed in still air is usually between 30 and 40 knots (55 and 75 kilometres per hour).

The daily weather report published by the Meteorological Office (London Rd, Bracknell, Berks RG12 2SZ) gives details of the wind, cloud, rain, temperature and pressure over much of Europe every six hours. If you are doing a migration study it is well worth subscribing to this, because it is often possible to make interesting suggestions about the origin of the birds one is recording by studying these maps. For example, the map reproduced on p. 122 by courtesy of the Meteorological Office (for 7 November 1974) shows good weather for winter visitors like Redwings, Fieldfares, Blackbirds and Starlings to leave Holland and Germany, where they are likely to have been passing, and to cross to England – at dusk in those areas the skies were largely clear above ground-level fog, there was a light following wind, and the temperature was falling for a frosty night.

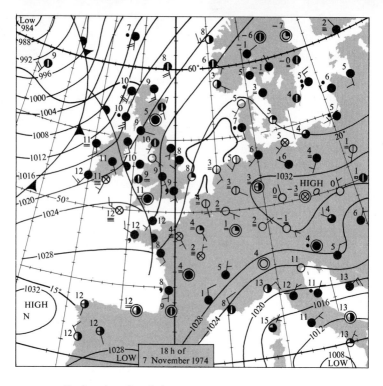

Explanation of symbols

CLOUD		WEATHER		WIND	
Symbol	Cloud Amount (oktas)	Symbol	Weather	Symbol	Wind speed (knots)
○	0	=	Mist		Calm
◑	1 or less	≡	Fog		1-2
◕	2	❟	Drizzle		3-7
◕	3	❟	Rain and drizzle		8-12
◐	4	●	Rain		13-17
⊖	5	✳	Rain and snow	For each additional half-feather add 5 knots	
◕	6	✳	Snow		
❶	7 or more	●▽	Rain shower		48-52
●	8	●✳▽	Rain and snow shower		
⊗	Sky obscured	✳▽	Snow shower		
⊗	Missing or doubtful data.	▲▽	Hail shower		
		⟋	Thunderstorm		

18 h of 7 November 1974

Any birds that did set off that night would have met cloud and rain in south-eastern England, and would probably have been seen mostly in Kent and Essex next morning. The distance into England from central Germany is about 680 kilometres, the birds' airspeed of, say, 35 knots (65 kms/hr) would have been increased to about 38 knots (70 kms/hr) by the following wind, so that they would have completed the journey in about ten hours, arriving an hour or two before dawn.

Weather maps can throw much interesting light on the results obtained in this way if you study them with care, and consider all the time the probable place of origin for the species concerned at that date. A check of distance against time (allowing for wind speed) can go a long way towards clinching a hypothesis.

Sky-watching

Particularly in autumn, but to some extent at all seasons, sky-watching can be a very productive way of tracking migration. The most spectacular sky-watching places are undoubtedly in other countries – at the Bosporus thousands of vultures, eagles and other birds of prey may be seen gracefully crossing the Dardanelles on their southward migration each autumn, and a similar but smaller passage may be seen at the Straits of Gibraltar. At Ottenby, on the southern tip of Øland (off the east coast of Sweden), hundreds of thousands of small birds pass in a continuous stream almost every morning during August and September. Britain is not so well shaped for concentrating the passage lines of birds in this way, but headlands like Selsey Bill (Sussex) have something of this effect. To a lesser extent still, the scarps of hills such as the Cotswolds and Chilterns, the Downs, major rivers and streams, and other natural features tend to concentrate the flight lines of low-flying migrating birds.

The technique of sky-watching is to find a good vantage point

(Opposite) Weather map issued by the Meteorological Office: 6.00 p.m., 7 November 1974

and to observe from it continuously for a period of time, recording all birds passing over, with time, number and direction. Analysis is often simplest if observing is done for a 'round' period of time, e.g. thirty minutes. The sky should be scanned continuously, and it is best, if possible, for a second observer to record the time and make the notes. A search should be made for high-flying birds, although usually it will only be possible to pick up ones that are visible to the naked eye. Birds that are observed to land or take off should not be included, and similarly you should exclude the random feeding flights of Swifts, Swallows and martins which zigzag across the area chasing flies. Everything else should be recorded – even unidentified birds. The final record might look something like this:

3 October. Clear, still, no frost.

0815	1 Skylark S.W.	0822	3 Skylarks W.
0816	3 Song Thrush W.	0822	4 Meadow Pipits S.W.
0816	1 Rook E.	0823	1 Pied Wagtail N.
0817	4 Meadow Pipits S.	0824	4 Pied Wagtails S.
0817	2 Pied Wagtails S.	0825	8 unidentified finches S.
0818	7 Meadow Pipits S.	0825	1 Blackbird N.
0821	3 Woodpigeons N.W.		

A record like this is probably reflecting a considerable amount of migration during the hours of daylight (especially larks, pipits, and wagtails in this case), and only a small amount of local movement. Local movement is likely to be much more predominant later in the day and at other seasons of the year.

Analysis requires only a ruler and graph paper. Total all the birds seen passing in each direction and plot an arrow on the graph paper, with length according to the number of birds involved (often 1mm = 1 bird will be appropriate).

Days when movement in one direction clearly predominates can be easily distinguished. Naturally they may well prove to be different days from those where numbers rise on ground counts

– if the sky-watch is successfully recording birds that are passing over, these birds will have been excluded from the ground counts.

Moon-watching

Passing mention needs to be made of the specialized technique of moon-watching. This involves watching the night sky against the outline of the full moon, through binoculars or a telescope. Patient observation is likely to be rewarded by the sight of a bird passing in front of the moon perhaps once every fifteen minutes in autumn. Similarly, birds may be seen at night in the light beams from many lighthouses. Identification by sight is usually difficult as the light passes so quickly, and you rely on calls, which of course can be heard anyway whether there is a light beam or not.

Daily records

Daily records for isolated areas, without comparison with other neighbouring areas as described above, can show periods of migration, and are of interest for first and last dates of migrants. But just because these are records for isolated areas, they are a less reliable source of information relating to the main periods of movement – above all else, the records will be heavily influenced by the suitability of the habitat for the particular species. Hence an inland lake or gravel pit is likely to yield plentiful information relating to the arrival and departure of Swallows, Willow Warblers, and Common Sandpipers, but be much less accurate about Nightjars, Blackcaps, or Starlings.

The most valuable results that are likely to be obtained from such daily records are not the freak early and late birds, but a general period of passage, and particularly the falling away of numbers in the autumn.

Coastal observations and bird observatories

Migration can often be observed in a spectacular way along the coast, when falls of many species occur around dawn, and there are good bird-watching opportunities. This is why a chain of bird observatories has been established all around the shores of Britain. There is a bird observatory at nearly all the best headlands and islands for seeing spectacular movements, but the observations that can be made from the other headlands and islands – and indeed even along the coasts in between – can still be very impressive at times, and on some occasions can excel those found at the observatories themselves.

From the scientific point of view the coastal observatories are probably less successful at recording the main movements of passerine birds than the inland schemes described above; but they do provide other kinds of invaluable information, particularly about interrupted passage and passage in poor weather conditions. In addition, the ringing of birds at these observatories has yielded results of incomparable value. The coastal observatories are also able to detect the presence of rare species in a way which has never yet been achieved inland. Besides the fun involved in just seeing these species, the observations and

studies made at the bird observatories have, in many cases, given us more information about the identification and habits of these rare species than has been obtained in their own breeding grounds, which are often far away in Siberia or the Middle East.

The information these observatories collect on the movements of waders, wildfowl, and seabirds is also of great value. The movements of birds that associate with the coast – a great variety of species from Common Scoter to Common and Arctic Terns – are likely to be accurately observed; and it is only records of the movements of the pelagic birds (the birds that do not normally come particularly close to land, like the phalaropes, shearwaters and petrels) that are likely to be distorted by vagaries of weather or the proximity of breeding colonies.

In view of the huge distances between the bird observatories (it is over 1120 kilometres between Fair Isle, off the coast of Scotland, and St Agnes in the Isles of Scilly), and the differences between locations (from remote islands to well-cultivated headlands), it is not surprising that each observatory has its own

speciality. Recent records from each observatory may be found summarized in *B.T.O. News* and 'Recent reports' in *British Birds* and these will quickly give an up-to-date indication of the special features of each of the observatories. In general, the east coast observatories produce a higher proportion of rare passerines than any of the other observatories; the southern observatories often record heavy movements of passerines, a large variety of waders and seabirds including many species rightly belonging further south. The western observatories pick up good movements of many British species in summer and winter, as well as the passage of more northerly birds; many of these western observatories, Cape Clear in particular, are outstanding as places for watching seabirds.

Since observatories are research establishments, it is not usually possible just to turn up at one and take part in its activities in the way you might turn up at a Youth Hostel or a Conservation Corps job. It is best to write in advance, booking a place. At most observatories the times when bookings are heaviest are April and August, and it may be necessary to book several months ahead if you can only go at that time. Places are often free at quite short notice for other seasons, although naturally the exact position will depend on which observatory you are considering. Addresses of the Bookings Secretaries are published in *B.T.O. News* and *British Birds*, or may be had by writing to the Secretary, British Trust for Ornithology, Beech Grove, Tring, Herts. Prices are usually in the order of £0·50 per night, unless full board is provided, in which case the charges may be around £1·50 a day. Once again, observatories vary in provisions made, and consequently in charges.

On arrival at the observatory you should meet the Warden, who will spend a few minutes showing you your place in a small dormitory and telling you about the observatory, and from then on you will be free to organize your time as you wish.

A typical observatory day starts at dawn, with a quick cup of tea; then you don your anoraks and scarves, and go off into the chilly twilight. Observers may break up into small groups to check over different areas of the island or observatory area, ready to spot every bird that moves. Most birds will belong to species that can be identified quickly and noted immediately in a field notebook; occasionally you will find a rarity, when you must stop and obtain a full field description, as described in Chapter 1. This may take half an hour or more. Depending on which observatory it is, one or more groups may do some early ringing, or go to the cliffs for a sea-watch. After a couple of hours or so in the field, the observers will return to the observatory for breakfast, and to compare notes. There may be points of identification to look up in the bird observatory library (most observatories have a wide variety of reference books, many of which may well be unfamiliar to the amateur and of great interest at any time). The rest of the day is likely to be spent in activities planned according to the observations of these first few hours: perhaps intensive ringing, a search rather farther afield, more detailed notes to confirm the identification of rarities, or another spell of sea-watching; or perhaps a full census will be taken, or nests checked on. There is almost always some maintenance work to be done in any spare moments, and copying up all the records takes many hours. At some point in the evening the Warden will write up the log, and it is usual for all the observers to be present for this, and for each to contribute his own observations from the day.

Even wet days may follow a similar pattern. It is important to be well equipped for going out in wind and rain, because rain may cause a heavy fall of migrants or drive seabirds in so close that wonderful views can be obtained of them.

Ringing can of course only be done by qualified ringers, but bird observatories undertake a great deal of training of new ringers. A stay at an observatory is also likely to provide a good opportunity to learn a lot of other ornithological skills from some of the best experts in the country. Ornithology is a very friendly hobby, and no beginner need be shy of mixing with, and learning from, any other observer at the observatory, no matter how much older or how distinguished the expert may be.

8   Sea-watching

It was at Dungeness Bird Observatory, in Kent, that I first learnt to sea-watch, in 1956. We sat for hours on the shingle in a bitter east wind on dismal April days, watching a light but varied passage of birds flying north-east up the English Channel, and turning the corner into the North Sea. There were several species of ducks (including sawbills), divers, an occasional tern and a few waders – notably godwits – passing reasonably close to the Point. They were all mixed up with an untidy array of shipping.

Most of the sea-watching I have done since then has been in south-west Ireland. There, you sit on the grassy cliff at the southern tip of a lovely island, and watch the huge Atlantic, rich blue and clear for forty miles, unbroken by anything except the lonely Fastnet Rock, the occasional back of a rolling whale, and the thousands of birds passing over.

When you go sea-watching you come to know a totally different group of birds. Many seabirds travel much greater distances than most small land-birds. Their food is in the sea, and they glide with ease on the sea winds. The Sooty Shearwater is a good example. This species breeds far south of the Equator – on islands and coastlines in the southern half of the Pacific. Each year in March and April (the end of its breeding season) it moves up the west side of the Atlantic. By the middle of the summer it is being seen all round the coasts of Britain, from the east coast of Scotland and north-east England to the south-west tip of Ireland. Late in our autumn it leaves our waters to go half-way round the world, back to where October is springtime.

I find it even more exciting to see a Great Shearwater, because it breeds only on a small group of islands in the middle of the southern Atlantic: the Tristan da Cunha group. When you see one of these, you really know where it has come from!

The commonest shearwater in Britain is the Manx Shearwater, which breeds round much of our coast. This is the shearwater you will see at least 999 times out of every thousand; but I cannot believe you will ever grow tired of seeing it, with its magnificent easy flight, rising and falling between the waves.

Besides the shearwaters, you are likely to see good numbers of divers, Gannets, Fulmars, auks, skuas, terns, ducks and waders, and if you are observant and very lucky, you may find petrels, phalaropes, or even one of the many species of albatross. And of course there are always the gulls, which are worth looking at carefully, because many species that do not breed here are seen in British waters. Which of these birds you see depends a great deal upon what part of the country you are in.

How you start

If you want to go sea-watching, you must go to the tip of a headland. Seabirds do not like to travel over land, and tend to keep only just in sight of it, cutting any corners they can: they do not usually follow the shore of a bay, but go straight across from headland to headland. There are still several major headlands in England where no one has done much systematic sea-watching. Of those that have been studied carefully, the coasts of Northumberland and Durham, Kent and Sussex (especially Selsey Bill), Portland Bill in Dorset, and several headlands in Ireland have probably produced the best results so far.

You might do best to start by going to stay at a bird obser-vatory. Observatories offering accommodation which have good opportunities for sea-watching are Spurn (Yorkshire), Dungeness (Kent), Portland Bill (Dorset), and Cape Clear Island (County Cork). Do not just turn up – write first and ask if you can go.

Even when you get to a headland, it is all too easy to fail to find the birds. Sea-watching technique is very important. You must have a good pair of binoculars, or a good telescope. If you are watching from a point not more than fifty feet above sea-level, you should be able to get excellent results with a telescope. If you are watching from higher points (do make sure that they are safe, and remember that grass is extremely slippery and you should never walk close to the edge on grass) binoculars are often better than a telescope, as you can move them about to scan the whole area so much more easily.

Half-hour stretches

Do not just wait until you can see a bird with the naked eye and then try to look at it with binoculars. Keep scanning the sea all the time. You should find a lot of birds a long way offshore that you would never have seen with the naked eye.

Sea-watching like this is hard work, and it is usually best to do half an hour only at a stretch; after a short break, you are ready for another half-hour. Avoid looking into the sun, or into water where the sun is reflected, and make sure your binoculars are clean and well focused. If you get a headache, stop at once, and see what is wrong: it is a sure sign you are straining your eyes. But if you sea-watch correctly you should have no trouble. And remember to take warm clothes; it is very cold on the cliffs.

Keen sea-watchers do not just look and try to identify what they see, they also make counts. You usually need a small team for this. One is the time-keeper who also keeps the record. Two others look and count. Sometimes one person counts half the species, and the other person the other half; sometimes one, with the telescope, counts birds a long way offshore, and the other, with binoculars, counts those closer in. They call out what they see and the record keeper writes it down. Someone on the cliffs listening in might hear this:

Record keeper: 'Coming up to 09.30. Ready to begin? Five, four, three, two, one, go.'

Telescope observer: 'Three Gannets east, one Cormorant east, five Manx Shearwaters west, six Fulmars west, two Gannets west.'

Binocular observer: 'Five Kittiwakes west, three Fulmars west, one Manx Shearwater east.'

Telescope observer: 'Big flock coming up, moving fast, west, now at ten o'clock, far out.' (Ten o'clock gives a bearing on an imaginary clock face on which twelve o'clock is straight out to sea.)

Binocular observer: 'Check. Moving low down, V formation. Look like auks.'

Telescope observer: 'Yes, I can see the beaks. They're Guillemots. About 40, west.'

Binocular observer: 'Three Kittiwakes west, one Manx Shearwater west, one Fulmar west, two Shags east . . .'

It is best to make counts for periods of exactly thirty minutes, because then one count can be compared with another; the time-keeper clearly has an important role to play here.

134

Identifying the birds

Identifying seabirds passing a long way offshore calls for different criteria from those you would use if you saw them close up at their nest sites, and so the ordinary identification books which are so good most of the time are less appropriate for this particular task.

At long range it is hard to distinguish colours, and even if you do, what you think you see may not be the real colour of the bird. A lot depends on what the light is like, so you must be prepared to identify seabirds without using colour; depending instead on size, manner of flight and general shape.

Gannets and gulls

Large birds which usually show a considerable quantity of white are gulls, Gannets and Fulmars. The terns, of course, may be almost as big as the smallest gulls and so need to be considered too.

An adult **Gannet** is, as a rule, easily identified; its wing-span is even larger than a Greater Black-backed Gull's, and it flies with a firm slow wing-beat. The shape of the wings is very characteristic – they have quite a sharp angle at the carpal joint – and the long

Gannet

bill and pointed tail make the body distinctive too. If you look at the shape you ought to be able to tell it from a Herring Gull (which is smaller anyway). Gannets are large, with very angular wings, bodies pointed back and front, and are easily the whitest seabird you will see.

The **Greater Black-backed Gulls** are almost as big as Gannets but a Gannet's back is white, and the dark back of a Black-backed Gull is usually visible. Besides, gulls have square-ended tails and their wings do not have a sharp angle at the carpal joint. The gull's wing-beat is as slow as a Gannet's, but the wing bends more as it goes down. The surest way of telling Greater and **Lesser Black-backed Gulls** apart at a distance is the speed of the wing-beat. A Greater Black-backed Gull takes a long time on a wing-beat, while a Lesser Black-backed Gull beats at about the same speed as a **Herring Gull** because it is about the same size.

The speed of the wing-beat is a feature that could be used more than it is in the identification of seabirds. So far, relatively little work has been done on it, though some observers (especially in north-east England) have timed the number of beats a minute on a stop-watch. It can be surprising how many beats are actually made in a minute – try it and see.

Herring Gull

136

Young Gannets and young gulls are more easily confused than the adults as they can both be mottled brown all over. Nevertheless, the differences of shape and manner of flight should separate them. It is only first-year Gannets that are brown all over; as they get older they have more and more blotches of white, until in their fourth or fifth year they assume full adult plumage. Young gulls get paler but do not become blotchy like a Gannet.

Kittiwakes and terns

Kittiwakes and **Black-headed Gulls** should not be confused with any of the three species just discussed. They are considerably smaller and less weighty birds, therefore they fly more buoyantly. The surest way to separate these two species is by their plumage markings, for they will often be indistinguishable in size and manner of flight. This means that at great ranges they can hardly be told apart, but fortunately they usually fly close inshore.

Kittiwake

The adult Kittiwake has completely black wing tips with no spots at all, and a clear grey back and mantle; the adult Black-headed Gull has either a black head (March–July), or a black spot behind the eye (August–February) and a white leading edge to the wing. Adult **Common Gulls** might be confused with Kittiwakes, but they have white spots at the tips of their wings like Herring Gulls. The upper wings of young Kittiwakes are boldly marked with a triangular black, white, and grey pattern; while young Black-headed Gulls have their wings mottled dark all over.

The various species of terns might be confused with Black-headed Gulls or Kittiwakes. Terns have forked tails – when you are close enough to see them! The larger terns (especially the **Sandwich Tern**) are about as heavy as a Black-headed Gull and their way of flight may be similar. **Arctic** and **Common Terns** (which cannot be differentiated at any great distance) generally fly even more buoyantly than Black-headed Gulls, and the **Black Tern** and **Little Tern** are more buoyant still – they rise and drop suddenly like feathers caught in a strong wind. All terns have long narrow wings, and, in summer, black caps; they commonly fly with their heads pointing downwards, whereas gulls hold theirs horizontally.

Common Gull

Common Tern

Fulmars

Fulmars have two distinct manners of flight, depending on the wind. In calm conditions they fly very low and very straight; if you see one approaching it often looks like a white ball, glistening in the light and going at a steady speed on a straight course. The wings move fast and stiffly, not dropping as low as a gull's wings. In wind, however, a Fulmar holds its wings rigid and glides for a while, interspersing this with short periods of flapping. Its gliding flight is a wheeling one, like a shearwater's, and so you sometimes see the upperparts and sometimes the under-parts.

The colour of a Fulmar can be confusing. In bright light it may appear almost pure white, with greyish wings. In soft light under rain clouds, however, it may seem a mottled sandy-brown above, although the breast (which really is white) always looks white. The light patch on the upper side of a Fulmar's wing is distinctive, as is the absence of neck – Fulmars always look as though they have a 'stiff neck', for the head joins the body thickly. There are also the variant 'blue' Fulmars, but these are rare.

Fulmar

Shearwaters

Manx Shearwaters will be found particularly on the west coasts, but occur in small numbers all around our shores except in the winter months. Normally they are easy to identify as in a light wind they glide for a couple of seconds after a short burst of flapping; these glides are usually angled on alternate wings, with, say, the left wing down on the first glide and the right wing down on the second. As the Manx Shearwater tips its back towards you, it seems entirely black; as it tips its under side, it seems mostly white.

The wings are held rigid when the bird is gliding, and they are long and narrow, with much less of an angle than most birds show. The wing-span is about that of a Herring Gull but the wings are narrower and the bird is smaller. Manx Shearwaters always fly low over the waves, and when flapping, the tips of the wings are bent down so they almost touch the water. In heavy seas, the shearwaters will completely disappear between the waves.

Manx Shearwaters, like most seabirds, can be difficult to identify in certain conditions. In a glaring light, for example, the under sides may seem as dark as the upper sides. When it is dead calm and the sea is still,

Manx Shearwater

they cannot shear and they fly low and straight with rapid flapping. Then you should distinguish them from auks by their wings being curved downwards (not held rigid), when beating, and their wing-beats are in fact not as fast as an auk's.

The only other shearwater you stand any real chance of seeing is the **Sooty Shearwater**. Books which describe it as being like a Manx Shearwater but dark all over are somewhat misleading, because it is quite distinct. Sooties are slightly larger than Manx, and seem much heavier, with slower wing-beats. Their wings are broader near the body and look much more tapered; this impression is increased by a fairly sharp angle on the wing. The tail is more noticeable too. The colour is not as black as the black of a Manx, and at considerable distances can be seen to be more that of black treacle or creosote. If the bird is very close (it has to be within a quarter of a mile if you are using ×8 binoculars), you may see a thin white stripe down the centre of the underwing. Some books mention this as a key identification feature; in fact it is variable from bird to bird and not distinguishable at many ranges where it is perfectly possible to tell a Sooty with confidence on size, shape and general colour.

Sooty Shearwater

The auks

The two large auks – **Razorbill** and **Guillemot** – approach Manx Shearwaters in size. And, like Manx, they are dark above and white below (though they have a white line on the upper wings if you can see them well). They fly very fast with extremely rapid wing-beats – the fastest you are likely to see – and with their wings held rigid even when beating. The tips of the wings do not seem to rise and fall nearly as much as in most birds. Auks usually fly straight and glide only briefly and occasionally. Unless you are close to them, you cannot tell Razorbills from Guillemots, so they are given the nickname 'Razor-gillies'. If you are within a quarter of a mile, you may be able to see the stubby-faced appearance of a Razorbill (which has a shortish bill) or the long pointed beak of a Guillemot. If you are so close that you can see the colours, the Guillemot is browner on the head.

The **Puffin** is the other common auk. It is noticeably smaller than the Razor-gillies – only about half the size of a Manx Shearwater. It has the typical manner of flight of an auk, but seems paler than a Razor-gilly and appears to have a very blunt face.

Razorbill

Guillemots

Puffin

Sea ducks

The **Scoter** is a common sea duck and might be confused with the larger auks. All ducks have rigid wings and fairly rapid wing-beats, and the speed of a Scoter's wing-beat is about the same as a Razor-gilly's. The easiest point to look for is that the Scoter is dark underneath as well as above; it is also larger and the wings are broader at the base and tapering, while the auk's are more uniform. Female Scoters are noticeably browner than males and at fairly close range their pale cheeks can be seen.

Common Scoters often fly in a V formation; auks occasionally achieve a good V and often fly in a cluster which has some hint of formation about it; shearwaters fly in loose formless groups.

Another species of duck which is very common, especially on the east coast, is the **Eider**. The drake of course is unmistakable, with its white neck and body with dark wings and tail. The duck looks a uniform dark brown, but it clearly is a large and heavy duck by the way it flies. **Brent Geese** may be seen in great numbers at passage seasons. Most other species of wildfowl may occur, and remember that the **Mallard** is regularly seen at sea too.

Common Scoters

The skuas

You may sometimes see one or two skuas while you are watching. The **Arctic Skua** is the commonest around Britain as a whole. It is about the size of a Manx Shearwater but it has a longer tail; if you see it very well you may even see that the central feathers are longer and cleft. This, however, is only visible on about one bird in four at sea-watching distances. The others, at this distance, seem to have longish tails with square ends.

Not all Arctic Skuas look the same. There are two types, known as 'light phase' and 'dark phase', and individuals can also fall between these two extremes. The colour of the under-parts varies from being a brown that is so pale it looks brown even at considerable ranges, to being as dark as a Sooty Shearwater; the upper side is always dark brown. There is usually a faint white flash towards the tips of the wings.

The Bonxie, or **Great Skua**, is not a close relation of the Arctic Skua. It is considerably larger and heavier, at least the size of a Herring Gull and coloured like a very dark young gull. The wings are broad at the base and taper to a sharp point, and there is a clear white

Arctic Skua

Great Skua

flash near the tip on the upper sides of the wings. This is essential to identification. The tail is short and square-ended.

Other species

Cormorants and **Shags** may sometimes fly quite far out to sea. Their all-dark plumage, long necks and slow flight should make them fairly easy to identify. Shags are less cumbersome than Cormorants, but this is not a safe feature to use on its own.

You should see waders passing fairly often. These are usually close inshore and then you will be able to identify them in the usual way as shown in the books. **Curlews** and **godwits** may fly further out, and sometimes in formation. They are easily identified as waders but you will only be able to tell the species if you see them well enough to get plumage markings.

Then there is the **British Storm Petrel**. This is a small seabird, like a half-size Manx Shearwater, but dark underneath with a white rump (if you see it well). At some distance it looks like a dark speck leaping from wave to wave, or it may seem to flutter like a

British Storm Petrel

huge butterfly. It generally keeps further offshore than the Manx Shearwater, and, being only the size of a Starling (though with longer wings), it is very hard to see without a telescope. An occasional **Swallow** or **House Martin** over the sea may trick you if you are not careful.

In northern and eastern waters in winter you are likely to see **divers** passing. When they are flying their hunched backs distinguish them from Shags and Cormorants.

Using features such as those described here, it should be possible to identify most of the birds you see passing, but no one must expect to be able to identify every bird: some must go unrecognized and therefore unrecorded, at any rate in any detail. But at a good sea-watching point, especially in spring and autumn, you should get hours of fascination watching an endless stream of these beautiful birds that swim and feed, flap and glide, riding the waves from end to end of the world.

9 Roosts

*Even at night there are a lot of things to find out about birds.
While they are asleep, birds are at the mercy of weather and
predators, and as they settle to sleep, they sometimes go through
strange rituals.*

This chapter describes an aspect of ornithology that is surprisingly neglected at present.

Birds need a safe place to sleep at night. In midsummer they do
not sleep long, and probably not deeply either; they usually
choose a perch near their nest site, and the female will sleep on
the nest itself. But as the nights begin to lengthen and grow
colder, it becomes more and more important that the birds
should have a warm safe place to spend the hours of darkness,
which, in midwinter, means about sixteen hours of every day.
They also seem to derive a great deal of advantage from gathering together.

Different species have different habits. Some roost alone
nearly all the year round, or during their time in our country –
all the warblers come into this category, as well as Robins,
Dunnocks and the tits. Others roost in large communal roosts
for part of the year – in the case of Starlings, some go to roost
almost every night of the year, while others join after the breeding season. The really big Starling roosts occur in winter when
the huge flocks of Starlings from across the North Sea gather
into very impressive roosts of a hundred thousand, or half a
million, or even over a million birds. No one has yet established

how far these wintering birds mix with our own native birds, or whether some of these large winter roosts are entirely composed of visiting birds. The same problem also arises with Blackbird roosts, where large numbers also arrive in autumn about the same time as the communal roosts (usually around a hundred birds in this case) begin to develop.

Roosts are fascinating to watch, because whether their numbers are breathtaking thousands or mere groups of twenty Reed Buntings or fifty Pied Wagtails, they are in each case more than you usually see of that species in any one place, and usually more than you can find in your home area by watching hard all day!

A wayside inn?

A roost may contain fifty birds, and night after night fifty birds come to settle in the bushes, only occasionally augmented by flocks coming in from outside. It would, however, be totally wrong to assume that those fifty birds are the same ones each night. Brian Dickinson and I studied a roost of Greenfinches of this size, during parts of four winter periods. Year after year we found that the particular birds using the roost changed night by night.

We would go to the roost, catch and ring a good proportion of the birds there, and let them go in time to see them settle back into the bushes for the night. Some we would see again a few days later, others we would not see again until the same season next year. Night after night we ringed new birds, and even when we had ringed a thousand individuals in this roost of 'fifty' we could still be sure we would catch unringed birds every time we went there!

The roost seemed to be no more than an inn, a stopping place on a daily wandering that our so-called resident birds seem to undertake throughout the winter months. Usually the birds we ringed did not wander far – the majority were recovered within

five miles of the roost. But one year when numbers were much
higher, recoveries came from much further away, showing that
the birds dispersed away from the roost far more widely, perhaps
back to the areas where they were born.

Where to look

Most species have their favourite type of roosting place, often in
thick bushes on top of a small hill. Of course, there are exceptional roosts! In 1961 a storm caused a freak movement in which
over thirty Shags appeared on the River Thames at Reading and
stayed there for several weeks. Shags usually roost on tall cliffs,
and as there were no cliffs at Reading they chose the top of the
gasometers! It was an incongruous sight to see these ungainly
deep-sea birds standing in a ring round the top of a provincial
town gasometer.

Setting aside such irregularities, the list on pp. 150–53 gives
some indication of the most usual seasons and places for each
species to roost.

Why do birds roost?

The roosting habit is hard to explain. Some birds seem to go to a lot of trouble to get to a communal roost, and some of them are involved in long and complicated displays when they arrive. It seems unlikely that this happens for no good reason. And yet there is no cut-and-dried, easy explanation. Indeed, it seems likely that there are different reasons, applying to different species and different times. Perhaps the four main reasons are these:

Warmth

Most roosts are in places where it is warmer than average during the night. Thermometers placed inside the bushes in a Greenfinch roost we studied showed that on average the inside of the bushes was warmer than the outside; and the sheltered wood where the roost was situated was itself 1·4 °C warmer than the surrounding area. This is a considerable advantage when the bird has to burn energy to keep itself warm for sixteen hours of

Roosting Habits of Our Most Common Species

Heron: at the heronry most of the year round. Small numbers usually.

Ducks, geese and swans: on islands or in fairly deep water.

Kestrel: no communal roost.

Pheasant: no communal roost.

Moorhen: no communal roost.

Coot: deep water.

Lapwing: winter; open fields, often up a hill.

Other waders: many waders do not sleep at night, but at high tide, whenever this occurs, and feed when the tide is down, whether it is dark or not. Autumn, winter and spring roosting places are sandbanks or fields above the high-water mark.

Gulls: autumn and winter; many gulls travel fifty to hundred kilometres each day to and from their roosts. Numbers at the roost can be very high. Most roosts are on large areas of open water, or sandbanks well away from the shore.

Woodpigeon: autumn, winter, spring; numbers greatly increased from the end of October to March by huge numbers entering Britain from across the North Sea to winter here. Roosts can be thousands strong, usually rather scattered, in thick rough woodland or in evergreen woodland.

Other doves and pigeons: mostly roost in small numbers, often around nesting holes or ledges.

Cuckoo: no communal roost.

Tawny Owl: no communal roost.

Swift: sometimes roost in the air – incredible as it may seem! Look for parties screaming across the evening sky at the end of July; as it grows dark these rise higher in the air and disappear. They can be seen descending just after dawn. This incredible observation is corroborated by watching the birds on radar and by aircraft pilots. The birds rise to around 1500 metres, where there are always quite strong winds, and with their exceptional wings they can remain airborne there with effortless gliding. Swifts, in fact, spend almost all their lives in the air except for nesting.

Swallows and Sand Martins: spring, and late summer; these two species both form very large and impressive roosts (up to 10,000 birds sometimes at the autumn peak), chiefly in reed beds over swampy water. They move to the roost singly or in small groups and are not easy to detect at this stage, but at the roost their movements are exciting to watch, as they swarm, rise, twist, and swoop in a frenzied display for perhaps half an hour before suddenly all settling and falling totally silent and unseen among the reeds.

House Martins: usually no communal roosts.

Carrion Crow: usually no communal roosts.

Rooks: Rooks roost in rookeries all the year round, but in winter the birds from the smaller rookeries tend to join those in the main rookery in the district, flying in substantial flocks. No long-distance movements.

Rook 'parliaments' (day-time meetings of thousands of Rooks, apparently strictly organized) are mysterious gatherings but not directly related to roosting.

Jackdaws: Jackdaws are often colonial birds; no communal roosts of birds from more than one colony seem to be formed.

Magpie: no communal roosts, although occasional groups of ten or twenty birds in thick hedges.

Tits: no communal roosts. In winter some birds roost in nest-boxes, and others who cannot find natural holes roost in hollows and cracks in the trunks of big trees out of the wind.

Wrens: occasional communal roosts in nestboxes. The fantastic total of over forty Wrens in one nestbox has been recorded on several occasions (the birds must be several layers deep!), but I have never had the luck to find such a roost myself. Usually no communal roosts.

Mistle Thrush, Song Thrush: large communal roosts are unusual. Occasionally they mix with other thrushes in small numbers.

Blackbirds: late autumn, winter, early spring; Blackbirds form noisy, scattered communal roosts, varying from ten or twenty birds into the hundreds, or occasionally over 1000 birds. They prefer rhododendron, evergreen hedges or trees, or other thick cover.

Redwing, Fieldfare: winter; Redwings and Fieldfares seem to roost communally for most of their time in our country, often flying several miles to the roost in straggling flocks of a few hundred birds. Most of the roosts are in very thick, impenetrable, thorn and bramble areas, well away from human habitation. All three other species of thrush are sometimes present.

Dunnock: no communal roosts.

Robin: no communal roosts.

Warblers: no communal roosts.

Meadow Pipit: autumn and spring migration periods; during this period Meadow Pipits spend several weeks in noisy, fidgety migratory flocks, and these can often be seen settling to roost together in rough grass. However, these are probably not roosts in the usual sense, in that the birds do not often gather from other flocks or other areas. Meadow Pipits sometimes associate with Pied Wagtails in their roosts.

Pied Wagtail: autumn, winter, early spring; Pied Wagtails, sometimes accompanied with migrating White Wagtails, gather from several kilometres around into roosts, which are in very varied locations. The commonest is in reed beds over marshy ground, but Pied Wagtails are also fond of exploiting man-made sites, such as the insides of greenhouses, warehouses and factories. At the roost the Wagtails are usually quiet and inconspicuous, although display flights occur occasionally; but they tend to gather in rather noisy pre-roosting flocks some short distance from the roost itself. To find the roost it is therefore important to wait until it is almost totally dark.

Starling: all the year round, particularly winter and migration seasons. The amazing numbers of birds in these roosts have already been mentioned. Most roosts are in thick thorn bushes, although town sites are also used. Birds gather into the roosts from many kilometres around, and stream towards the roosting area in tight-knit flocks rushing by with a hiss of wings; individual flocks approaching a big roost can number many thousand birds. Films have been taken of the birds leaving these roosts at dawn, as seen on radar, and this shows that they spread out in a series of rings, as flocks depart at approximately five minute intervals. Birds in the roosts are packed extremely closely together.

Greenfinch: winter and spring. Most roosts number fifty to 100 birds, although occasionally larger roosts can be formed. Strong preference for thick rhododendron or other evergreen bushes. Often on a hill top.

Goldfinch: no communal roosts except family parties.

Linnet: autumn, winter, spring. Roosts can number 500 to 1000 birds, usually in areas of thick gorse, or alternatively forestry plantation or young hawthorn, often on a hill top. Impressive flighting at times. Flocks gather some kilometres away and can be traced moving up to the roost.

Bullfinch: no communal roosts, although ten or twenty may gather in a thick hedge.

Chaffinch: late autumn, winter, spring; some Chaffinches may roost in small numbers in thick hedges, but often large roosts are formed, usually in woodland. Birds enter singly or in small groups, but fly in calling regularly from many kilometres around, and are therefore easy to track. Much calling at the roost, but few displays.

Yellowhammer, Reed Bunting: roosts of tens or even a hundred or more can be found in thick hedges (Yellowhammers) or marshy ground (Reed Bunting), the birds moving in quietly from several kilometres around.

House Sparrow: most House Sparrows roost close to where they spend the day, but when numbers in an area are large, these may gather into roosts of some hundreds, often in thick hedges.

darkness in mid-winter. The bird has only eight hours to collect its food, and although many birds arrive at the roost with their crops bulging with stored food (and their weight substantially increased with it), they will consume all this store during the night. Warmth can therefore be an attraction in the case of the smaller roosts gathering from a few miles around, but some roosts (e.g., for gulls) are clearly not warmer, and many involve such long flights that the loss of feeding time, and the energy spent flying there and back, must more than outweigh the advantage of the warmth. So warmth is certainly not a total answer.

Safety

A sleeping bird is obviously easy prey for a predator, whether rat, hawk, or man. If large numbers of birds are sleeping together, the alarm cry of the first bird disturbed or taken can be a warning to the others in the neighbourhood.

On the other hand, the sheer act of gathering in one place advertises their presence, and often Sparrow Hawks or owls move in when a roost gathers in an area. I have seen a Sparrow Hawk quartering a Starling roost at dusk, and even when it has taken a bird, only a few birds in the immediate vicinity were disturbed. Once they are settled many roosting birds sleep so soundly that they are unlikely to respond to warning calls. There seems therefore to be doubtful advantage in terms of safety at a roost.

Population estimates

The intense displays at the roosts are considered by C. W. Wynne-Edwards* to be 'epideictic' displays enabling the birds to estimate the numbers of that species within the area. He postulates that this would have the effect of inducing some birds to leave an over-populated area, and also of reducing the propor-

*See *Animal Dispersion in Relation to Social Behaviour*, Oliver & Boyd, 1962.

tion of birds that nest, or the number of eggs they lay, when populations are high. Certainly such reductions do occur, but the work Brian Dickinson and I did on a Greenfinch roost showed clearly (see p. 147) that we are not dealing with a 'closed' population at any time, and Wynne-Edwards' theory demands that the population should be closed in this way, at any rate for some time. His book, *Animal Dispersion in Relation to Social Behaviour*, is fascinating reading, however, and poses a lot of important questions. Certainly the similarity of the flights of birds with the dances of midges or the swarming movements of herring shoals is remarkable, and may indicate a certain degree of parallelism in their purposes.

Scrounging ideas for feeding areas

It has been suggested by I. Newton that the birds going to a roost have the advantage of being able to follow others back to successful feeding areas next morning, since feeding time in winter is so precious that there would be a very great advantage in being able to get to a good area quickly. If this is the case, some of the birds entering a roost are 'parasitizing' on those birds there that have found good feeding areas.

This is an ingenious suggestion, and may well have a lot of truth in it, but again it is only a partial explanation. Even for finch roosts in winter, it is not at all clear that the birds leave in different directions from those in which they arrived; it would seem, if the theory were valid, that one would be able to detect a considerable 're-orientation' of the birds visiting the area for the first time, into the feeding areas of the birds who were already 'in the know'. More field-work is needed on this point. But this theory certainly does not account for the long-distance movements, or the summer and autumn roosts.

There is a lot of explaining still to be done about roosts, and it is a topic of more than academic importance. The thick and the marshy areas so often used for roosting are gradually being whittled away by farmers and builders. Up to now the birds seem to have been able to find alternative sites when they have lost a good roosting area. What will happen to them when they cannot find suitable alternative roosting areas?

Doing surveys on roosting

Unquestionably ringing is a particularly valuable tool in roost studies, but there are a lot of good field-workers who are not ringers. Even without ringing there is plenty still to be found out.

Map the roosts in the area

Firstly, it is important to map as many roosts as possible in the area. While some may escape detection, it is likely that suitable roosting sites may be found at intervals of less than a kilometre in each direction, and these may be used by a variety of species. Regular studies of these roosts, and the numbers of birds entering them, can give very valuable information about the winter or passage population levels of these species. No study of a local area would be complete without this information.

To find the roosts, two main techniques are necessary. For species that fly to the roosts in flocks, it is possible to map the direction of flight observed at different points and project these lines until they cross; it is likely that the roost will be near the point of intersection. Except when there are substantial obstacles to avoid, such as high hills, birds fly in straight lines directly towards the roost, and are therefore easy to track.

For the other species, it is a matter of observing likely places for roosts. You may know where these places are already from your knowledge of the area, or it may be necessary to study carefully the 1 : 50,000 O.S. map to see where to look. Most birds gather to roost as the light begins to get weaker, but the actual time of settling varies with the species. Greenfinches settle early, Blackbirds late, and gulls only settle long after dark. Generally speaking, to be sure of finding a roost in a given area it is important to be in the area, quiet and inconspicuous, for the last hour of daylight, and not to leave until all the colours have faded.

Research on explanations for roosting

It has already been pointed out (see page 155) that Newton's theory needs considerably more field-work, and much of this can usefully be done by observation, if a suitable roost to study can be found. It would be important to do the work at a roost where the birds can be seen entering and leaving over a considerable distance in all directions. Detailed counts of those coming and leaving from each direction, correlated with known feeding areas some miles around, would be very interesting. It is not yet known how much the wind affects the direction of approach or departure, nor how far the birds need to orient themselves on leaving a roost in an unfamiliar area. These complications would have to be allowed for.

Further studies of the temperature differences inside and outside roosts would also be valuable. Furthermore, working very quietly in the dead of night, it might be possible to establish how close birds are to each other in the roosts, and how much they increase the temperature advantage with their own body radiation.

Finally, day-by-day counts of the numbers of birds in a particular roost, correlated with all other known facts about population levels in the area, might help to throw more light on the extent to which roosts are used as a 'wayside inn', and what conditions trigger off large-scale movements of the 'guests'.

Roost studies have a long way to go. Some important things are waiting to be found out. And finding them out is going to give someone a lot of pleasure.

10   Surveys Round
and About

No one can make a good bird watcher who does not notice where birds are and what they eat. Some bird watchers are also very interested in botany, and enjoy studying the plant life of the area at the same time.

This chapter describes several studies that can be usefully made round and about. While most surveys require you to watch a particular area regularly, some can be rewarding when done all over the country on a quite random basis.

The keen observer is likely to find many different special surveys to make from time to time. In each case it is important to begin by asking yourself three questions:

1. What do I want to find out?
2. How am I going to collect the information?
3. How am I going to sort it out afterwards?

I have seen too many cases of enthusiasts collecting large quantities of information that they could not use – partly because they were missing a vital point of observation that they had not thought of at the beginning, and partly because the records were so badly laid out that they could not dig out the points they wanted afterwards. Wordy diaries are not convenient. Think how you can set out the records in a table or a set of tables. Think how you can present the results in maps, block graphs, pie charts or other clear forms. Plan all this first, and record your information in a standard form to suit this scheme.

Here are four kinds of surveys that are well worth making.

Albinism

It can be rewarding to study albinism – the unusual white patches sometimes found on birds. All species of animals (even human beings) can produce albinos. An albino has all feathers or hair pure white, and the iris of the eye is pink. You may be lucky enough to see a pure albino bird (an albino House Martin swirling across a deep blue sky is a beautiful sight). But far more commonly you will find birds that have patches of white feathers in unusual places.

A survey of albinism can show which species suffer from albinism most frequently, whether albinism happens more in town centres, suburban districts, or the country, and also, by comparing how many albinistic birds you see in the autumn with those seen in the spring, whether albinistic birds survive as well as other birds. (Are they more conspicuous to predators? Are they attacked by other birds of their own species?)

You will need to record where and when you saw each bird, and which parts of its body were abnormally white. Albinism is often lop-sided, but sometimes it can appear symmetrically. Beware then of confusion with species that are 'meant' to have areas of white on them – do not mistake, for example, a female Reed Bunting with white outer tail feathers for a supposed female House Sparrow with albinistic tail feathers! You must, of course, be as certain as ever that your identification is right and that the white patches are abnormal.

The results of a survey of albinism done by David Torr at Nottingham are given on p. 160 for interest. It does not follow at all that you will obtain the same results. He did not consider the question of whether the albinistic birds were found in town, suburban areas, or country. Nor did he give any detailed analysis by season. This could be interesting because feathers cannot change colour once they have grown, so the numbers of albinistic birds should stay much the same as the numbers of other birds from the end of moult (about the end of September) until the beginning of the next moult (not earlier than June). A

Albinistic birds seen in 1969

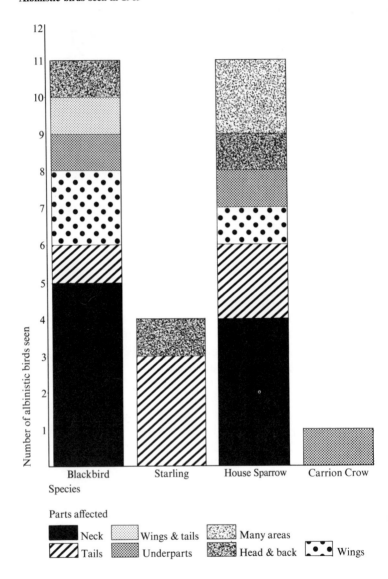

bird that is albinistic one year may not be albinistic the next year – albinism appears to have many different causes. Sometimes it seems to be genetic, being passed on from parents to offspring; at other times it appears to be the result of a skin injury at the point where the white feathers later grow, or of poor diet at the time of the moult.

A survey of albinism can usefully be made over large areas – while you are away on holiday, as well – and there is still a lot to be found out about this subject.

Habitats

Every species of bird prefers to live and feed in one particular type of area, and this is called its habitat. As you get to know more about birds, you begin to acquire an idea of the type of habitat each species favours, but a careful study can be both interesting and rewarding. It can be interesting because it can reveal many details that the casual observer may overlook, and it can be rewarding because it may allow you to learn enough to be able to re-plan an area in order to make it much more favourable for birds.

It is well known that birds are adapted for the sort of place they live in – ducks with webbed feet and well-oiled feathers to help them keep warm while swimming, or birds of prey with hooked beaks for tearing their prey, and so on. But in fact the way each species fits into its particularly favoured area (its 'ecological niche') is much more subtle than this. It is certainly not enough, for example, to say that a Willow Tit is a bird of damp woodland. If it is to be able to breed in the area, it needs some rotting tree stumps in which it can dig out its nesting hole. Nor is it enough to say that Chaffinches like stubble fields where they can pick up grain that has fallen from the harvester (the chaff that they get their name from) – fallen corn or fallen beech mast is the favoured food in autumn, but in spring they are birds of hedgerows, feeding their young on insects and grubs. An ideal habitat for a species may therefore include more than one type of area, or more than one main feeding source, so that different aspects can be explored at different times.

A hedge is not just a hedge

Looking at a habitat carefully can be a long and complicated business. A hedge is certainly not just a hedge. You must ask what sort of bushes grow in the hedge. Is it along a ditch or a bank? How thick is it and how tall is it? Is the bottom of the hedge sprayed with weedkillers or allowed to grow thick natural vegetation?

How often is the hedge cut back? Has it been layered, or has it been cut by hand, or hacked back with a rotary saw mounted on a tractor?

The bird life to be found in a hedge will vary enormously according to the answers to these questions. Some modern farms have thin sprayed hedges which are trimmed back mechanically every year, and which support almost no bird life at all. On the

other hand a thick varied hedge which has probably been a field boundary for two hundred years, and which is occasionally layered and otherwise merely gently trimmed back, can be one of the most exciting and highly populated areas to be found.

Similarly with waterways. There is an enormous difference between polluted and unpolluted water, there is an enormous difference between slow sluggish water and fast running water, and there can also be an enormous difference between water that dries up in drought and areas that are always wet. A quick look on one occasion will not give a good description of the habitat. The habitat, just like the bird life, needs to be studied for a considerable time.

Rapidly changing habitats

Some particularly fascinating bird watching can be done in areas that are changing rapidly. We started bird watching at the new Ratcliffe on Soar (Notts.) Power Station before it was ready to generate electricity; at that time the ground was still hard from

the rolling of bulldozers, and the plantations that were meant to screen the station had only just been put in. It was rare indeed that we could see more than two or three species of bird on the site. But it was worth making the records, for within four years the total species list for the site had risen to 49 species, and the young plantation was already supporting a good breeding colony of Linnets, as well as nesting Lesser Whitethroats, Grasshopper Warblers, Dunnocks, Song Thrushes, Pheasants, and several other species. In years to come this may become a really good bird-watching area. New gravel pits can yield similarly fascinating results, as we discovered on a new part of the Attenborough Gravel Pit in Nottinghamshire (see p. 80).

Naturalists with a good understanding of habitat requirements need to influence architects and land agents to persuade them to plant new areas with vegetation that will soon support a rich and varied wild life. Far too often the architects think of planting sycamore and black pine, on the grounds that they are fast-growing trees. They may plant in native hard woods like beech and oak as well, claiming that this will help wild life later on. Unfortunately this type of mixture is unlikely to harbour much wild life of any sort for twenty years, and is unlikely to be rich in wild life for much longer than that. Native shrubs like hawthorn and field maple, and even 'weeds' like bramble and nettle, ought to be introduced to these bare areas to give a quickly grown and varied lower layer of growth; the trees can come up above this later on.

Suggestions of this sort will carry most weight if they are based on some good field-work. The B.T.O.'s Common Birds Census is providing a lot of useful data along these lines for breeding birds, but a lot more work needs to be done on preferred habitats for many common species at other times of the year. The scheme suggested here is a simple beginning. Those keen on the botanical side ought to extend this into far greater detail.

Habitat survey

This survey will help you appreciate which areas are most important to conserve for each species, and which types of habitat
ought to be introduced to an area to increase the bird life. Many
areas of land around factories, offices, and schools are quite
unnecessarily bare and empty of shrubs, trees, and birds. A good
appreciation of preferred habitats can give an insight into the
type of development that could be done to make a site interesting within as little as five years, or in a few cases even sooner
than that.

First decide what habitats you want to study and how you are
going to divide them, and also make a list of the species you are
specially interested in. You will be kept busy recording the habitats of the birds you see and it is a good idea to limit the number
of species being studied. Our Swindon survey was limited to
eighteen varied species, all of which were fairly common but not
likely to be found in huge numbers. Naturally, only perched
birds can be recorded.

The block graphs shown on pp. 166–7 from the Swindon survey demonstrate very clearly the striking differences in the
preferred habitats of common species. The survey could usefully
be divided into different seasons, to establish whether these
preferences vary at different times of year, and much more
detailed analysis of the habitats generally could be revealing.

Bird song

Bird song is an indication of the health and condition of wild
birds; passerines only sing when their pituitaries are producing
enough androgen to stimulate a certain amount of sexual
behaviour, and when there is enough food for the males to be
able to afford the time for singing. A survey of song periods can
therefore throw light on the birds' health as well as being very
good training in noticing, and identifying, the songs heard. It is

Habitats where Chaffinches were seen, Wiltshire, 1974-75 Winter

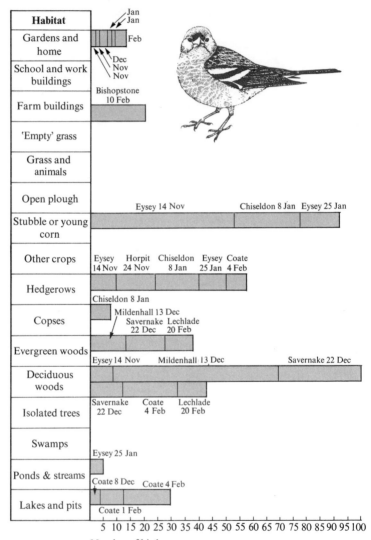

Number of birds seen

Habitats where Bullfinches were seen, Wiltshire, 1974-75 Winter

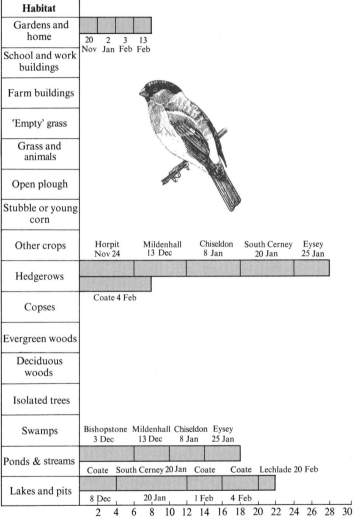

Number of birds seen

important to distinguish between other calls and song (not all that easy in the case of tits, Starlings or Tree Sparrows) and it is wise to make some note of the intensity of the song. Is the song given intermittently and shortly, as so often in autumn, or is it almost continuous and accompanied with other displays, such as song flights, as is more common in spring? Results are probably best presented in calendar form, as in the examples shown on p. 169.

A bird's day

Anyone who is used to bird watching in woodland knows how common it is to find small parties of several species of birds moving through the wood, feeding actively as they go. Commonly these parties will include Blue, Coal and Marsh Tits, Treecreepers, Long-tailed Tits and Goldcrests. They will be keeping together with high-pitched contact notes – and although each species has a quite distinctive call, there is a considerable similarity between the contact notes of all of these.

As far as I know no one has yet done any careful research on this feeding technique. A lot needs to be found out:

How far do the parties travel?

Do they keep to the same route each day?

Do they feed in different habitats along the route?

Does the route always finish where it began?

Do the birds keep on the move all day long?

The answers could tell us some important things about the extent and type of woodland needed to build up a good population of these species.

Similarly, some interesting work could be done on the activities throughout the day of much more sedentary birds, like Robins, Dunnocks, Blackbirds and House Sparrows. Many of these seem to have very precise rhythms, visiting particular parts of a garden for feeding only at certain times of day, and yet relatively little work has been done to catalogue their day or measure the accuracy of their timing.

Birds heard singing, February 1975

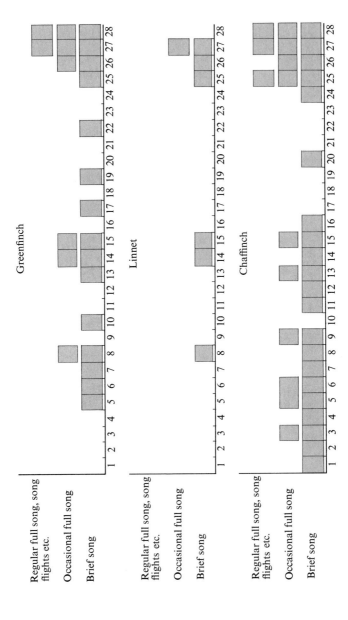

Greenfinch

Linnet

Chaffinch

11   Collections

Egg collecting is happily becoming a thing of the past. Apart from its cruelty there can be no doubt that it has done much damage to the populations of many of our scarcer species. There are still those who wilfully break the law, although, as explained in Chapter 4, the law is perfectly reasonable and quite precise, but prosecutions are becoming more frequent and sentences more severe.

But although you should never collect eggs, or imitate the naturalists of the last century by shooting birds, there are other things that can be collected and that can be very instructive.

Pellets

Pellets regurgitated by owls can sometimes be found under large trees. (Many species make pellets – it is possible that almost all species do so on occasion – but it is much more difficult to find or to recognize the pellets of smaller birds.) When an owl feeds, it swallows the bird, mouse or beetle complete with feathers, fur, or wing-cases. As birds do not have teeth, the food passes to the crop without the digestive process having begun (with humans our saliva begins to digest our food as we chew). In the crop, it is ground by strong muscles, usually churning it with small stones the bird has swallowed for the purpose. The food then passes to the stomach, where digestion begins, while the crop forms a pellet of the roughage that the bird later regurgitates. It follows therefore that a pellet is a wholesome thing to handle, and it is unlikely to contain more bacteria than were to be found on the living animal that was eaten, and it will be free of most of the gastric juices.

One collector known to me found half a dozen Tawny Owl pellets and soon established that that particular bird was feeding on House Sparrows – he laid out a row of fourteen sparrow skulls, each complete with the beak, and below these he sellotaped in neat rows most of the leg bones of the same birds; the smaller bones were too broken for easy identification. Other pellets may produce rows of wing-cases of beetles, or the teeth of small mammals that can then be identified by reference to *The Handbook of British Mammals.**

Birds found dead

Frequently dead birds are found that have been run over, or killed by a fox or a cat. When the body has been fairly severely damaged, it may be possible to collect a wing or some striking feathers. If the wings are pinned neatly on to a card, they can begin a most informative collection. With so many of our smaller birds it is the colours on the wings that indicate the age and sex of the bird. The difference in colouring between male and female Linnets in autumn, for example, is particularly in the width of the white webs on the wing feathers. Faced with just one bird, or one wing, it can be hard to decide whether the white fringe is 'narrow' (female) or 'broad' (male). Reference to a few specimens will quickly establish the difference.

Ornithologists may also like to preserve the bodies of any casualties found in good condition. There are two ways of doing this. One is the way used by taxidermists in museums, the other is a quicker and simpler method. Naturally the taxidermists' method produces the better specimen, and, done by an expert, the result can be superb. However, for amateur collections it is doubtful if the time and effort involved is worth it.

A bird in a museum is a skin – it has been carefully cut open,

*H. N. Southern, *The Handbook of British Mammals*, Blackwell, 1965.

and all the bones and flesh removed, and the fat scraped off the skin. It is then filled with cotton wool and re-sewn. Glass beads are used for eyes. Some weird and monstrous birds have been displayed in museums where the taxidermist was ignorant of the posture of the living bird – Dunnocks with long bulging necks, and divers standing proudly erect like penguins when in reality they usually shuffle along on land with their breast-bone touching the ground. Similarly, the paint that is used on the 'soft parts' may be very wide of the mark from the real colour. (The 'soft parts' are, strangely enough, the hardest parts of the bird – the beak, legs and feet; but these parts lose their natural colour soon after death, whereas feathers only fade slowly over a period of many years.) Many of these birds in strange postures have been faithfully painted by artists equally ignorant of the living bird, resulting in many of the misleading colour illustrations to be found in the cheaper bird books. It is among other things in their insight into the posture and mannerisms of the living bird that the really great artists like Robert Gillmor, Roger Tory Peterson, Archibald Thorburn, Donald Watson, Charles Tunnicliffe and John Leigh Pemberton have excelled.

Since professional taxidermy is so difficult, the merits of the quick way are considerable. This involves nothing more than injecting the entire body with formaldehyde, and allowing it to dry out. The procedure will usually take only a few minutes and the specimen will last for years.

The formaldehyde quickly stiffens all the tissues, and once set they cannot be moved again. Hence before injecting the formaldehyde the body should be set in the posture required for display. Our way is to lay the bird on its back with the wings pinned out, since this allows you to study more of the plumage than any other posture; it does however lead to a slight flattening along the back. Sometimes it is more desirable to set the bird in a supporting frame so that a swimming or walking posture is obtained. Large birds may need to be injected on the side that will be temporarily inaccessible (while in the jig drying out) before being finally set in position.

A very small bird like a Wren will only need to be injected into its stomach; the formaldehyde will diffuse from there through all the tissues of any importance. On the other hand a heavy bird like a duck or swan will need to be injected into all 'meaty' tissues, including the muscles along the wing and the legs, those of the shoulder, neck and even around the head. Furthermore, heavy birds will probably dry out slowly, over a period of a week or two, and will need re-injection at intervals during this time. Sometimes the support of stout wire is needed inside the neck.

Once the bird has dried out it can be taken out of its jig, because it will be quite stiff, and can be displayed in any suitable glass cabinet, preferably not in full sunlight. A faint smell of formaldehyde will linger, especially in hot weather, but so long as the bird has been thoroughly treated this will not be noticeable outside the cabinet.

It is best to use a high concentration of formaldehyde (40 per cent if possible); any cheap hypodermic syringe will do. It is essential to remember that formaldehyde is poisonous. It must be kept in a safe place clearly labelled '40 per cent formaldehyde. POISON'. Care should be taken not to allow any to touch the skin or enter the eyes; if it does, wash off immediately under a running tap. (Severe cases would need a doctor, but I have never had need to consult one yet, in nearly ten years of using this method in schools.) The most likely danger is that the end of the needle will become jammed with a particle of a feather, and as you press on the syringe the needle is freed, and formaldehyde is sprayed around. No one should ever crouch near to watch the process, and the person doing the injecting should stand back. The fumes of formaldehyde, if any is released into the room, are very pungent and will quickly bring tears to the eyes; no harm will come of inhaling them for a brief period.

Any corpse that is treated in this way will gradually dry out, and therefore shrink. So it is important to use the minimum amount of formaldehyde to preserve the specimen. It seems that about one millilitre of 40 per cent formaldehyde per ten grammes of

Species	Usual body weight	Likely total of 40 per cent formaldehyde required
Chiffchaff	7 g	1 ml
Dunnock	14 g	1½ ml
House Sparrow	30 g	3 ml
Skylark	50 g	5 ml
Song Thrush	80 g	8 ml
Blackbird	100 g	10 ml
Wild Mallard	2000 g	200 ml

body weight is about correct. The table above gives an idea of the amount of formaldehyde required for some typical birds.

Besides birds, mammals and fish can be preserved by this method. The shrinkage in these is more obvious because there are no feathers to hide it. It is true that a roach can come to look more like a kipper, and a pike like an old log, but moles, foxes and squirrels make lovely specimens.

12 A Note about Ringing

Bird ringing is a particularly valuable way of studying birds, since it is usually the only way we have of being sure that we are looking at the same individual that we saw before; it is also the only way we have of keeping track of a bird when it has flown away from the area where we are working. About half a million birds are ringed in Britain every year, and each one of these has a unique number on its ring, like a car registration number plate. And as with cars, too, large numbers of birds are also marked in many other countries of the world, but every ring in the world is individually distinguishable. This is essential since British-ringed birds have now been found in every part of the world, including Australia, South America, and the eastern coast of Russia by the Pacific Ocean, and birds from almost every other country have been found in Britain.

To ring a bird, you must, of course, catch it, and this could be dangerous for the bird. Ringing is therefore strictly controlled by law, and you can only become a ringer by a proper course of training.

How to be trained

The only way to begin training for ringing is to get in touch with a bird ringer and ask if you can be taken on. The ringer will be someone who is doing it as a hobby – no one is employed as a ringer on a full-time paid basis – and if you are taken on, he will not be paid for teaching you. Naturally you may be asked to pay the cost of what you do – usually three to five pence for each ring – and probably also a subscription to a Ringing Group to help buy or renew the equipment. The ringer will be spending many hours of his free time ringing, and will expect only serious-minded learners who are prepared to turn up as often as they can, and to work hard when they are there. No one should ever begin ringing until he has become a good field-worker, used to doing the sort of surveys described in this book. Learn your birds first, and the ringing after.

If you have not got to know a local ringer while you are doing local surveys, the B.T.O. will supply the address of one or two who live fairly near you. There are only about 1000 fully trained ringers in the country – this means there are about twenty-two head teachers for every ringer – so you may have to travel a bit to find one.

You may begin training at the age of fourteen if you can find a ringer who will take you on then. You will need a T-permit (Training) from the B.T.O. office and a special handling licence from the Nature Conservancy Council – but the ringer will tell you how to get these. You can ring only under direct supervision until you are sixteen. At sixteen or more, if you are adequately trained, you can have a C-permit, which allows a certain amount of ringing on your own; but a C-permit is only given to people who have ringed a lot of birds in training (usually between one thousand and two thousand birds), who know their birds well, and who have shown themselves to be reliable in every way – sensible with the birds and nets, polite with the public, and careful about writing up the records. There is a lot of writing to do, because there is no point catching and ringing a bird unless you collect a lot of information while you have got it.

The youngest age for having an A-permit, which means being a fully trained ringer, is eighteen. The whole training course is bound to be long. Adults who begin ringing, and are not therefore slowed down by the age restriction, must normally expect to spend at least two years from the beginning of training until they get an A-permit. Although it is possible to catch and ring the necessary number of birds in a few weeks of intense activity, you cannot be considered properly trained in less than one complete year, for it is essential to see the different plumages and to study moult, and also to experience the empty days as well as the full ones. Two years is a more reasonable time.

Does it hurt the bird?

Ringing done properly does not hurt the bird at all. But nets and traps in the wrong hands can cause a lot of suffering. The trained ringer learns the rules and the techniques, and with a careful ringer casualties are almost totally unknown. The ring goes round the 'leg' (which is really the tarsus) without squashing the skin, but without being too loose either. The bird flies away a few minutes after being caught, unharmed and perfectly fit. If it had a parasite when it was caught, the ringer will probably have taken it off! Rings come in many sizes, to suit each bird. The ring itself is very light. There are nearly 25 rings to a gramme in the size used on most small birds. You could say this must feel like wearing an extra sock on one foot, but there is another big difference which means that the weight must matter even less than this – a bird changes weight much more than we do. We do not lose a stone of weight each night while we sleep, or put it on again during one day, nor do we usually put on three or four stone in cold weather – but a bird's weight changes on this scale. A female bird in spring with several eggs developing inside her is carrying as much extra weight as several hundred rings.

Why do we ring birds?

Ringing helps the birds! Of course, it does not help the bird that has the ring on, but the information we get from ringing provides the solid factual information that conservators need for protecting a species, or birds in general. How much notice would the Government, or big business, or land developers, or some ruthless farmers, take of us if we said 'You mustn't carry out this plan because we watch the birds there and we think they fly away to other countries from there (but we don't know), and we think they don't live as long as they used to (but we don't know)'? Ringing gives the facts on these points and these cannot be argued about. From the ringing scheme, we know for sure where birds come from and go to, and how long they live.

Since bird populations can be at the mercy of many unexpected catastrophes, it is important that we ring a good sample of all our birds, even common ones, every year. Some catastrophe could easily affect only part of a population: only the young birds, for example. Field observation would be unlikely to reveal this. A changed pattern of ringing recoveries would.

What other information do you get?

While the bird is being handled, note is usually made of its age and sex, wing length, weight, moult, parasites and any abnormalities. Occasionally special studies are made – my club was once asked to wash the birds' feet to discover if they were carrying the cysts of nematode worms. Migrant warblers arriving in Britain have been found with pollen on their beaks – examination has shown that this was orange blossom pollen, proving that the birds had fed the night before in the orange trees on the Mediterranean coast.

It is often possible to tell a bird's age and sex when you have it in the hand, but not in the field. Robins, for example, can be aged by the colour inside the beak, but they cannot be sexed at all. Song Thrushes can be aged by the shape of the tail feathers, and Goldfinches can be sexed by the extent of the crimson feathers on the forehead. These are just a few examples. Calculations of the proportion of young birds to old birds ringed each year can obviously produce a lot of information about the breeding success in that year.

Most small birds do not live very long, and so a large proportion of the birds caught are expected to be first-year birds. If we can re-trap the birds in later years, or if enough are found dead and reported by the finder, it is possible to work out the normal life expectancy, and to see how this may change from year to year. You cannot make sensible conservation plans without this information.

Wing lengths give us a guide to two types of information – sex and subspecies. As soon as a bird is old enough to fly properly its wing feathers are fully grown. In species where sexes cannot be distinguished, such as Robin, wing length can be a useful guide, although not an infallible proof of sex – Robins with wings 76–8 mm long are probably males, and those around 70–72 mm are probably females. It is not a safe test for any one bird, but if all the results are plotted on a graph it does give a good guide to the overall proportions of each sex in the sample you have been ringing.

The weight is a very important measurement to take from a bird. Birds are weighed on specially accurate spring balances (usually while they are comfortable inside a cloth bag). Some birds put on a lot of weight before a long migratory flight, to give them the energy they need for the flight. If we catch a Sedge Warbler which only weighs about 12 g in autumn, we do not expect it to begin its migratory journey just then; on the other hand, one that weighs perhaps 21 g when it is caught is ready for departure, and might well be leaving the country the same night as it is caught. Similarly very light-weight birds caught in spring are probably ones that have just completed a long flight. In spring, females often weigh more than males, because of the development of their ovaries and the eggs they are carrying inside them, and a female Dunnock, for example, can be distinguished for the first time from a male.

It is only in the last ten years that we have begun to have any thorough knowledge of when birds moult, or of which migrant birds moult in Britain and which moult in their winter quarters. A bird that is moulting is likely to be feeling out of sorts, and certainly will be less efficient in the air than one with good new feathers. The stage of moult can therefore be important to the subsequent survival chances of the bird that is caught. Worn feathers can tell us that we are handling an adult bird, and new feathers that we are handling a first-year bird, in the case of many species where there is no other clear way of distinguishing these on plumage characteristics.

Some ringers with interest in insects make special studies of bird parasites, while other ringers who are doctors take blood samples. These studies have given some useful information relating to the survival of many species.

A detailed case history can thus be built up on each bird as soon as it is caught; all the information is then carefully filed. Often birds are caught again, usually by the same ringer, and valuable additional information can then be added to the file showing how the bird is faring during the year. The information is also stored centrally, and a detailed analysis carried out every year; special studies are made of all the European ringing results from time to time. All recoveries of birds ringed in Europe, for example, will, one day, be handled on the same computer.

How do I find out more about ringing?

The best source of information about the ringing scheme is a booklet published by the B.T.O. in 1974, called *Bird Ringing*. More detailed information on the results of the ringing scheme are published every year in a special report, also available from the B.T.O. The results of various analyses are published in several different journals, but most of them appear in *Bird Study* and *Ringing and Migration*. Ringing tends to be a rather glamorous aspect of field work, and television programmes and news items concerning it are rather more frequent than one would expect considering how few people are working on it.

13 Books, Journals and Societies

Books

I hope this book will help every reader to become a good ornithologist, but it will not be enough on its own. To begin with, I have tried to avoid saying again things that have already been said well in other books. Secondly, an ornithologist cannot work in isolation, but he must know what others are doing, and he must cooperate with others if his work is to have any real value. Hence the need for some comment on books, journals and societies.

The list of recommended books on page 187 is a personal selection of books that I have found to be of most value in helping new enthusiasts to become well informed, as well as making very good reading. A quick look at the shelves in any library or bookshop will soon reveal what a lot of other books have been published about birds. Some are very good, but perhaps a bit pricy for the ordinary pocket, and best borrowed from a library, read and enjoyed, and returned. The books listed here are all superb books, written by people who are expert within their own areas, well produced, and usually cheap considering what they offer. Where possible, I recommend buying them all.

Journals

In ornithology, as in most sciences, it is not possible to be entirely well informed by reading just books. Most of the new research results are published in the journals, and some of this never finds its way into book form. A journal is quite different from a magazine. A magazine is easy to read, and may be worth keeping for the fun of it. A journal is solid reading, but is always worth filing carefully, because material is built up gradually.

The bibliography that follows here indicates just some of the reports that have been published in recent years covering the work discussed in this book alone. Back numbers of the journals referred to can be consulted in big libraries and are held by some local ornithological societies. Copies can also be read at the Edward Grey Institute Library in South Parks Road, Oxford, and at the Tring offices of the B.T.O.

There are three main journals in British ornithology, as well as a few more specialist publications. *Ibis* is published by the British Ornithologists' Union, and contains many longer papers, concerned not only with British birds, but with ornithological findings from all over the world. *Bird Study* is the journal of the B.T.O., and contains papers relating particularly to the work of the B.T.O. and its members, as well as a certain number of other papers of more general interest. Most, but not all, of the reports in *Bird Study* relate to British birds. *British Birds** is an independent non-profit-making publication of very long standing. It carries miscellaneous papers concerning birds found in Britain, but in so far as it specializes it does so in the areas of identification, general habits, and rare birds. The more specialist publications include *Wildfowl*, the annual report of the Wildfowl Trust, and the annual reports of all the bird observatories and the local ornithological societies throughout the country. Another specialist publication of great importance is the *Proceedings* of the International Ornithological Congress, held in different countries of the world every four years. Naturally the papers published here relate to birds the world over. The publication of the R.S.P.B., *Birds*, is strictly speaking a magazine, but it is very well produced and the reports are very authoritative; they only differ from being scientific papers in that they generally summarize work that has been previously published elsewhere, rather than presenting new information for the first time. Copies of *Birds* are well worth collecting and treasuring along with the other journals.

---

*The journal *British Birds* can be obtained from Macmillan Journals Ltd, 4 Little Essex St, London WC2R 3LF.

All the other journals mentioned can be obtained from the society which publishes them: the addresses are given on p. 185.

Reading list: papers in journals

Batten, L. A., 'Bird Population Changes for the Years 1970–71', *Bird Study*, 19, 241–8.

Batten, L. A., 'Bird Population Changes for the Years 1971–2', *Bird Study*, 20, 303–7.

Bell, B. D., Catchpole, C. K., Corbett, K. J., and Hornby, R. J., 'Relationship between Census Results and Breeding Populations of some Marshland Passerines', *Bird Study*, 20, 127–40.

Coulson, J. C., 'Mortality and Egg-production of the Meadow Pipit with Special Reference to Altitude', *Bird Study*, 3, 119–32.

Dickinson, B. H. B., and Dobinson, H. M., 'A Study of a Greenfinch Roost', *Bird Study*, 16, 135–46.

Dobinson, H. M., and Richards, A. J., 'The Effects of the Severe Winter of 1962/63 on Birds in Britain', *British Birds*, 57, 373–434.

Dobinson, H. M., 'The Inland Observation Point Scheme', *Bird Migration*, 2, 3.

Goodacre, M. J., and Lack, D., 'Early Breeding in 1957', *British Birds*, 52, 74–83.

Hickling, R. A. O., 'Inland Wintering of Gulls in England, 1963', *Bird Study*, 14, 104–13.

Holyoak, D. T., 'Breeding Biology of the Corvidae', *Bird Study*, 14, 153–68.

Lack, D., 'Cuckoo Hosts in England', *Bird Study*, 10, 185–202.

Lack, D., 'A Quantitative Breeding Study of British Tits', *Ardea*, 46, 92–124.

Lack, D., 'Radar Evidence on Migratory Orientation', *British Birds*, 55, 139–58.

Lack, D., 'Seaward Flights of Swifts at Dusk', *Bird Study*, 1, 37–42.

Lister, M. D., 'Lapwing Habitat Enquiry 1960–61', *Bird Study*, 11, 128–47.

Monk, J. F., 'Breeding Biology of the Greenfinch', *Bird Study*, 1, 2–24.

Monk, J. F., 'Past and Present Status of the Wryneck in the British Isles', *Bird Study*, 10, 112–32.

Myres, M. T., 'Breeding of Blackbird, Song Thrush and Mistle Thrush in Great Britain (Breeding Seasons)', *Bird Study*, 2, 2–23.

Newton, I., 'Breeding Biology of the Chaffinch', *Bird Study*, 11, 47–68.

Peal, R. E. F., 'Distribution of the Wryneck in the British Isles 1964–1966', *Bird Study*, 15, 111–26.

Phillips, J. H., 'Distribution of the Sooty Shearwater around the British Isles', *British Birds*, 56, 197–203.

Reynolds, C. M., 'Census of Heronries 1969–1973', *Bird Study*, 21, 129–34.

Sage, B. L., 'Albinism and Melanism in Birds', *British Birds*, 55, 201–25.

Sharrock, J. T. R., 'Little Swift in County Cork: A Species New to Ireland and Britain', *British Birds*, 61, 160–62.

Simmons, K. E. L., 'The Advertising Behaviour of the Great Crested Grebe', *Bird Study*, 1, 53–6.

Simpson, J. E., 'Swifts and Sea-breeze Fronts', *British Birds*, 60, 225–39.

Snow, D. W., 'Breeding Biology of Blackbird, Song Thrush and Mistle Thrush in Great Britain (Clutch Size and Nesting Success)', *Bird Study*, 2, 72–84 and 169–78.

Summers Smith, D., 'Breeding Biology of the Spotted Flycatcher', *British Birds*, 45, 153–67.

Taylor, S. M., 'Common Bird Census, Some Statistical Aspects', *Bird Study*, 12, 268–86.

Tubbs, C. R., 'Analysis of Nest Record Cards for the Buzzard', *Bird Study*, 19, 97–104.

Winstanley, D., Spencer, R., and Williamson, K., 'Where Have All the Whitethroats Gone?', *Bird Study*, 21, 1–14.

Libraries

Most local libraries are well stocked with books on birds, and a few of the big ones also retain copies of the journals. On the other hand there may be many parts of the country where it is not possible to obtain copies of the journals except by travelling a considerable distance, unless the local ornithological society maintains a library of its own. The B.T.O. maintains a lending-library service for its members. The most complete ornithological library in the country is maintained in Oxford by the Edward Grey Institute in conjunction with the B.T.O. This is not a lending library, but a visit to South Parks Road in Oxford will be rewarded with many fascinating hours reading in the library itself. It has all the major publications from all over the world. The best specialist bird bookshop in the country is run by the Scottish Ornithological Society at 21 Regent Terrace, Edinburgh. Write for a book list. Books can be ordered by post, and will be sent almost by return. They have a magnificent stock, all at standard prices. It is well worth sending for their list, which currently mentions over 300 different bird and natural history books.

National societies

Membership of national societies naturally entitles you to receive copies of the journals free of charge and immediately upon publication, and most societies also send newsletters to members between publication of the journals. There are often other advantages of membership, apart from the obvious one of being involved and of contributing to their work. The addresses are as follows:

British Ornithologists' Union,
c/o Bird Room,
British Museum (Natural History)
London S.W.7.

The B.O.U. is a learned society that many bird watchers like to join when they have become competent ornithologists.

British Trust for Ornithology,
Beech Grove,
Tring,
Herts.

The B.T.O. is open to anyone interested in the scientific study of birds. Anyone who is interested in the type of survey described in this book will find that the B.T.O. offers him more of interest than any other society.

Wildfowl Trust,
Slimbridge,
Gloucestershire.

The Wildfowl Trust is, naturally, particularly interested in wildfowl, both in the superb collections maintained by the Trust, and in the wild.

Royal Society for the Protection of Birds,
The Lodge,
Sandy,
Bedfordshire.

The R.S.P.B. is concerned with protection in the widest sense, including making the public interested and informed about our bird life. Besides running many reserves and being actively concerned in law enforcement, the R.S.P.B. produces many excellent films and other material.

Local societies

In almost all areas of the country there are local ornithological societies, but the few parts that are not covered have natural history societies that take an interest in ornithology. Lists of all the societies and their addresses can be obtained by writing for information from the R.S.P.B. or the B.T.O., or the Council for Nature.

Local societies vary a lot in their character and functions, but generally speaking they have three main areas of activity:

(a) They organize meetings during the winter months, which are often accounts of interesting expeditions made, or studies of particular species.

(b) They organize field outings, either within their own areas or by coach to more distant areas. These give an opportunity to see interesting birds, and to meet other bird watchers.

(c) Most important, they collect records of the birds in their areas, and publish them in an annual report. Here there is a great deal of variation between societies. There are some where the report is a tedious and incomplete collection of raw facts, and it is doubtful if it is worth the effort and cost of producing it. Where a lively society has been fortunate enough to get a good editor, the report can contain some very valuable and fascinating analyses of the records obtained in the area, and can be as valuable a document as some issues of the national journals.

It is much to be hoped that all new keen ornithologists will therefore join as many of these as possible, and in particular, the British Trust for Ornithology, the Royal Society for the Protection of Birds and their local ornithological society. If they can also support good causes like the County Naturalists' Trusts, that work hard to conserve all the interesting areas within each county, this is strongly to be recommended.

List of recommended books

Atkinson-Willes, G. L., *Wildfowl in Great Britain*, H.M.S.O., 1963.

Bang, P., and Dahlstrom, P., *Animal Tracks and Signs*, Collins, 1964.

Batten, J., Flegg, J., and others, *The Birdwatcher's Year*, T. & A. D. Poyser, 1973.

Benson, S. Vere, *The Observers' Book of Birds*, Warne, revised ed., 1972.

Bruun, B., *The Hamlyn Guide to Birds of Britain and Europe*, Hamlyn, 1974.

B.T.O. Field Guide, *Bird Ringing*, B.T.O., 1974

B.T.O. Field Guide, *Binoculars, Telescopes and Cameras*, B.T.O., n.d.

B.T.O. Field Guide, *Nestboxes*, B.T.O., n.d.

B.T.O. Field Guide, *The Nest Records Scheme*, B.T.O., n.d.

Burton, M., *The Life of Birds*, MacDonald Educational, 1972.

Campbell, B., *Oxford Book of Birds*, Oxford University Press, 1964.

Campbell, B., and Ferguson-Lees, J., *A Field Guide to Birds' Nests*, Constable, 1972.

Cramp, S., Bourne, W. R. P., and Saunders, D., *Sea Birds of Britain and Ireland*, Collins, 1974.

Dorst, J., *The Migrations of Birds*, Heinemann, 1962.

Ennion, E. A. R., and Tinbergen, N., *Tracks*, Oxford University Press, 1967.

Fisher, J., *Thorburn's Birds*, Michael Joseph and Ebury Press, 1967.

Fisher, J., revised by Flegg, J., *Watching Birds*, T. & A. D. Poyser, 1974.

Fitter, R. S. R., and Richardson, R. A., *Pocket Guide to British Birds*, Collins, 1966.

Fitter, R. S. R., *The A.A. Book of Birds*, Reader's Digest, 1969.

Flegg, J., *Discovering Bird Watching*, Shire Publications, 1973.

Fogden, M., and Fogden, P., *Animals and their Colours*, Peter Lowe, 1974.

Gooders, J., *Where to Watch Birds*, Deutsch, 1967.

Hanzak, J., edited by Campbell, B., *The Pictorial Encyclopedia of Birds*, Hamlyn, 1967.

Harrison, C., *Nests, Eggs and Nestlings*, Collins, 1975.

Heinzel, H., Fitter, R. S. R., and Parslow, J., *The Birds of Britain and Europe*, Collins, 1972.

Hoeher, S., and Reade, W., *Birds' Eggs and Nesting Habitats*, Blandford, 1974.

Hollom, P. A. D., *Popular Handbook of British Birds*, H. F. & G. Witherby, 1971.

Lack, D., *Swifts in a Tower*, Chapman and Hall, 1956.

Lack, D., *Enjoying Ornithology*, Methuen, 1965.

Lack, D., *The Life of the Robin*, H. F. & G. Witherby, 4th ed., 1965. Fontana (Paperback).

Lockley, R. M., *Ocean Wanderers*, David & Charles, 1975.

Lorenz, K., *King Solomon's Ring*, Methuen, 1952.

Matthews, G. V. T., *Bird Navigation*, C.U.P., 2nd ed., 1968.

Merne, O. J., *Ducks, Geese and Swans*, Hamlyn, 1974.

Murton, R. K., *The Woodpigeon*, Collins, 1965.

Newton, I., *Finches*, Collins, 1973.

Ogilvie, M. A., *Ducks of Britain and Europe*, T. & A. D. Poyser, 1975.

Parslow, J., *Breeding Birds of Britain and Ireland*, T. & A. D. Poyser, 1973.

Perrins, C. M., *Birds*, Collins, 1974.

Peterson, R. T., Mountfort, G., and Hollom, P. A. D., *A Field Guide to the Birds of Britain and Europe*, Collins, 3rd ed., 1974.

Reade, W., and Hosking, E., *Nesting Birds, Eggs and Fledglings*, Blandford, 1967.

R.S.P.B., *Wild Birds and the Law*, R.S.P.B., 1971.

Saunders, D., *Seabirds*, Hamlyn, 1971.

Scott, P., *Coloured Key to the Wildfowl of the World*, Wildfowl Trust, 1965.

Sharrock, J. T. R., *Natural History of Cape Clear Island*, T. & A. D. Poyser, 1973.

Sharrock, J. T. R., *The Natural History of Cape Clear Island*, T. & A. D. Poyser, 1973.

Sharrock, J. T. R., *Scarce Migrant Birds of Britain and Ireland*, T. & A. D. Poyser, 1974.

Soper, T., and Gillmor, R., *The New Bird Table Book*, David & Charles, 1973.

Sparks, J., Soper, T., and Gillmor, R., *Owls, their Natural and Unnatural History*, David & Charles, 1973.

Thomson, A. L., *A New Dictionary of Birds*, Nelson, 1964.
Tinbergen, N., *The Herring Gull's World*, Collins, 1953.
Wynne-Edwards, C. W., *Animal Dispersion in Relation to Social Behaviour*, Oliver & Boyd, 1962.

Out of print books still worth obtaining:
Jourdain, F. C. R., and Kirkman, F. B., *British Birds*, Nelson, 1930.
Voous, K. H., *Atlas of European Birds*, Nelson, 1960.
Witherby, H. F., Jourdain, F. C. R., Ticehurst, N. F., and Tucker, B. W., *The Handbook of British Birds*, H. F. & G. Witherby, 1940, 5 vols.

Index